A Handbook of
Modern Rhetorical Terms

A Handbook of
Modern Rhetorical Terms

Linda Woodson
Texas Tech University

National Council of Teachers of English
1111 Kenyon Road, Urbana, Illinois 61801

Book Design: Tom Kovacs, interior; V. Martin, cover.

NCTE Stock Number 20199

Library of Congress Cataloging in Publication Data

Woodson, Linda, 1943–
  A handbook of modern rhetorical terms.

  Bibliography: p.
  Includes index.
  1. Rhetoric—Dictionaries. I. Title.
PN172.W6   808'.003   79–17400
ISBN 0-8141-2019-9

Contents

Preface

The joy of being in the second generation of what is called the "new rhetoric" is that the importance of the fruitful work done in rhetoric and in composition during this century no longer needs defending. We know that a knowledge of rhetoric—historical, theoretical, pedagogical—can give us the needed confidence of sound scholarship. We know that understanding the long and important history and tradition of rhetoric can give us a sense of the dignity and significance of what we do, a sense that cannot be gained from "bag of tricks" techniques. As Imlac declares in Samuel Johnson's *Rasselas:* "those who have kingdoms to govern, have understandings to cultivate."

Knowing the importance of the rapidly multiplying scholarship, however, does not make the task of staying informed any less bewildering, as the authors of *Teaching Composition: 10 Bibliographical Essays* have so recently and excellently made clear. My book then is an attempt to bring together in one place the myriad of words that have been added to rhetoric and composition in this century. This attempt can be only a beginning; there must be many more gatherings of words like this one in the future. But it is my hope that these words and definitions will make that task somewhat easier.

I have compiled this vocabulary of modern rhetoric from textbooks, from theoretical studies, from pedagogical and curricular explorations, and from plain practical studies. The terms are primarily twentieth century, but I have included some classical terms which are still widely used and which the reader might often encounter. I have tried to be as inclusive as possible, but the responsibility for deciding if a word should be included is my own. The listing of the terms is alphabetical. Following each term is a definition, often in the words of its originator. A bibliographical reference is cited for the first use of the word or for its principal use in composition, and this is often followed by a quotation showing the word in context. Finally, any other bibliographical references which indicate changes or extensions in meaning the word may have undergone are included, and sometimes an example is given.

An Appendix classifying the words according to subject headings has been provided as a cross-reference to facilitate an understanding of the functions of the words. The book concludes with an Index of names of authors cited in the definitions.

Earlier in this Preface I said that I have tried to be as inclusive as possible. This aim has resulted in the inclusion of some words that are, to be blunt, jargon. Rhetorical study, it seems, has shared in the guilt of coining imprecise, pretentious terms when older terms are satisfactory. I trust that the users of this handbook will join me in the hope that these terms will not be perpetuated and that our profession will continue its leadership in eliminating doublespeak.

To make proper acknowledgments would be impossible because the list of people to whom I owe thanks is endless, beginning of course with the names of all the scholars whose works are cited in the text and including all the teachers and students whose efforts made the work of those scholars possible. I shall have to be content with thanking Jim Corder and Gary Tate for providing the initial impetus for this book. My thanks go also to Paul O'Dea and to the Editorial Board of the National Council of Teachers of English for their help.

Linda Woodson

Annotated, Alphabetical List of Rhetorical Terms

A

abduction. Also called *retroduction.* The process in the logic of the discovery procedure of working from evidence to hypothesis, involving a back-and-forth movement of suggestion and checking. In this process two pieces of data could be explained by a hypothesis, the validity of which could be corroborated by the finding of another piece of data. If the third piece of data is true, then the hypothesis is probably true. Since the question remains of what suggested the hypothesis, abduction differs from deduction, which follows the pattern of asserted antecedent to consequence. John P. Day, *Inductive Probability* (New York: Humanities Press, 1961), pp. 66ff. I. M. Bochenski, *The Methods of Contemporary Thought* (Dordrecht, Holland: D. Reidel Publishing Co., 1965), pp. 92ff. For a discussion and model, see James L. Kinneavy, *A Theory of Discourse* (Englewood Cliffs, N.J.: Prentice-Hall, 1971), pp. 143-44:

> In the process of abductive discovery, two separate pieces of data, d_1 and d_2 could both be explained by a hypothesis H_1; if this hypothesis were true, further data should exist which would corroborate the existence of H_1; this corroborative data is cd_3. Similarly d_4 and d_5 could be explained by H_2 and its existence could be corroborated by the finding of cd_6. Supposing the corroborative data to have been found, H_1 and H_2 both suggest a common explanation E. If E were true, then it would suggest another hypothesis H_3, which could be corroborated by cd_7.

accessibility. The relative ease or difficulty with which meaning can be derived from a sentence. For a discussion, see W. Ross Winterowd, "The Three R's: Reading, Reading, and Rhetoric," *A Symposium in Rhetoric,* ed. William E. Tanner, J. Dean Bishop, and Turner S. Kobler (Denton: Texas Woman's University Press, 1976), p. 53.

act. The element of the dramatistic framework called the Pentad—
act, scene, agent, agency, and purpose—that answers the question, What was done? for a thought or an event. Kenneth Burke,
A Grammar of Motives (New York: Prentice-Hall, 1945):
" 'Dramatistically,' the basic unit of action would be defined as
'the human body in conscious or purposive motion.' " (p. 14)
See *dramatistic framework* and *Pentad.*

addition. In composition, a structural principle of building on the
noun, the verb, and the main clause of a sentence by adding
qualifiers or modifiers, or of building upon the lead or thesis
sentence of a paragraph by adding modifying sentences. Francis
Christensen, "A Generative Rhetoric of the Sentence," *College
Composition and Communication* 14 (October 1963), 155-61:

> For the foundation of such a generative or productive rhetoric I
> take the statement from John Erskine, the originator of the Great
> Books courses, himself a novelist. In the essay "The Craft of
> Writing" (*Twentieth Century English,* Philosophical Library,
> 1946) he discusses a principle of the writer's craft which, though
> known he says to all practitioners, he has never seen discussed in
> print. The principle is this: "When you write, you make a point,
> not by subtracting as though you sharpened a pencil, but by
> adding."

Example: "He shook his hands, a quick shake [noun cluster],
fingers down [absolute], like a pianist [prepositional phrase]."
—Sinclair Lewis.

addressed writing. The characteristic of writing that it must be
concerned with an audience, created by the idea that persuasion
implies an audience. Kenneth Burke, *A Rhetoric of Motives*
(Berkeley: University of California Press, 1969), pp. 38-39:
"Thus by a roundabout route we come upon another aspect of
Rhetoric: its nature as *addressed,* since persuasion implies an
audience." (p. 38)

addressee. The person being addressed in discourse. Roman
Jakobson, "Linguistics and Poetics," *Style in Language,* ed.
Thomas A. Sebeok (New York: John Wiley & Sons and M.I.T.
Press, 1960), pp. 350-77.

addresser. The speaker or writer in discourse. Roman Jakobson,
"Linguistics and Poetics," *Style in Language,* ed. Thomas A.
Sebeok (New York: John Wiley & Sons and M.I.T. Press, 1960),
pp. 350-77.

affective domain. The area of educational goals describing changes in interests, attitudes, and values, and the development of appreciation and adequate adjustment. For a discussion, see Benjamin S. Bloom et al., eds., *Taxonomy of Educational Objectives* (New York: David McKay Co., 1956). See *Bloom's taxonomy*.

agency. The element of the dramatistic framework called the Pentad—act, scene, agent, agency, and purpose—that answers the questions, How? and By what means? for a thought or an event. Kenneth Burke, *A Grammar of Motives* (New York: Prentice-Hall, 1945). See *dramatistic framework* and *Pentad*.

agent. The element of the dramatistic framework called the Pentad—act, scene, agent, agency, and purpose—that answers the question, Who did it? for a thought or an event. Kenneth Burke, *A Grammar of Motives* (New York: Prentice-Hall, 1945). See *dramatistic framework* and *Pentad*.

aim of discourse. The effect that the discourse is intended to achieve in the listener or reader. I. A. Richards, *The Philosophy of Rhetoric* (New York: Oxford University Press, 1965), pp. 23-43. James L. Kinneavy, "The Basic Aims of Discourse," *College Composition and Communication* 20 (December 1969), 297:

> It is the intent as embodied in the discourse, the intent of the work, as traditional philosophy called it. Is the work intended to delight or to persuade or to inform or to demonstrate the logical proof of a position? These would be typical aims.

See James L. Kinneavy, *A Theory of Discourse* (Englewood Cliffs, N.J.: Prentice-Hall, 1971).

anaphora. A rhetorical figure in which the same word is repeated at the beginning of successive phrases, clauses, or sentences. Example: "Theirs not to make reply, / Theirs not to reason why, / Theirs but to do and die."—Tennyson, *The Charge of the Light Brigade*.

antithesis. A figure that makes use of contrasting words, phrases, sentences, or ideas for emphasis. Generally the contrasting ideas are found in parallel grammatical structures. Examples: "Man proposes, but God disposes."—Thomas à Kempis; and "Corrupted freemen are the worst slaves."—David Garrick.

apostrophe. A figure in which a person or an abstract quality is directly addressed, whether present or not. Example: "Stern Daughter of the Voice of God! / O Duty! if that name thou love"—Wordsworth, "Ode to Duty."

argumentation. Also *persuasion.* A classification or form of discourse having as its function to convince or persuade an audience or to prove or refute a point of view or an issue. Argumentation uses induction, moving from observations about particular things to generalizations, or deduction, moving from generalizations to valid inferences about particulars, or some combination of the two as its pattern of development. The traditional modes of discourse—narration, description, argumentation, and exposition—are believed to have been first identified as such by Alexander Bain in *English Composition and Rhetoric* (American edition, New York: D. Appleton & Co., 1890). Traditionally three forms of appeal have been identified in argumentation: logical (*logos*), emotional (*pathos*), and ethical (*ethos*). Logical argument is a clear, appropriate progression of thought or evidence and a conclusion. Emotional argument evokes emotional responses in the audience. Ethical argument rests upon the response to the speaker or author as someone to be trusted. The traditional parts of an argument are as follows:

exordium—the beginning, in which the author gains attention or establishes credibility or both;

narratio—background or context for the discussion;

propositio—proposition, thesis, or chief theme;

partitio—delineation of the steps to be followed in the discussion;

confirmatio—proof and evidence in support of the proposition;

confutatio—refutation or citing of inadequacies in the opposing viewpoint;

digressio—digression, related items or arguments;

peroratio—conclusion summarizing key points or calls for action.

Most rhetoric textbooks have good discussions of argumentation. In addition, see Stephen Toulmin, *The Uses of Argument* (Cambridge: At the University Press, 1958); Richard D. Rieke and Malcolm O. Sillars, *Argumentation and the Decision Making*

Process (New York: John Wiley & Sons, 1975); and Chaim Perelman and L. Olbrechts-Tyteca, *The New Rhetoric,* trans. John Wilkinson and Purcell Weaver (Notre Dame, Ind.: University of Notre Dame Press, 1969). See also *Rogerian argument.*

arrangement.   See *dispositio* and *form.*

assembled topic sentence.   A composite topic expressed in fragments of several sentences running through a paragraph. Richard Braddock, "The Frequency and Placement of Topic Sentences in Expository Prose," *Research in the Teaching of English* 8 (Winter 1974), 287-302. Example:

> In some ways, *we are paying interest on a giant credit card.* When the inventors of the automobile began the age of rapid transit, they were building up charges for which all of us are responsible. *This credit card was the drain on our nation's energy resources,* and *the interest is long lines at the gas station.*

See *topic sentence.*

assertorial tone.   The quality of a statement as to both carrying meaning and asserting truth. Statements vary as to the degree to which they can be affirmed or denied, ranging from *heavy* tone, characteristic of the literal statement that is easily affirmed or denied, to *light* tone, a simple association between two images. Philip Wheelwright, *The Burning Fountain* (Bloomington: Indiana University Press, 1968), pp. 92-96. Examples: *light:* "An idea / like a canary / singing in the dark / for appleseed and barley."—Carl Rakosi, *A Journey Far Away; heavy:* "An idea is like a canary singing in the dark for appleseed and barley."—Wheelwright, p. 95.

asyndeton.   The omission of conjunctions between words, phrases, or clauses. Example: "eye for eye, tooth for tooth, hand for hand, foot for foot."—Deuteronomy 19:21.

attitude of rhetoric.   The particular state of mind of a speaker or writer in discussing a subject and which forms a part of his or her message. Nine of these attitudes, as identified by Weathers and Winchester, are: confidant, judicious, quiet, imperative, impassioned, compassionate, critical, angry, and absurd. Winston Weathers and Otis Winchester, *The Attitudes of Rhetoric* (Englewood Cliffs, N.J.: Prentice-Hall, 1970).

B

base clause. In the cumulative sentence, the main clause, which is likely to be stated in general, abstract, or plural terms. Francis Christensen and Bonniejean Christensen, *Notes Toward a New Rhetoric,* 2d ed. (New York: Harper & Row, 1978), p. 28: "The main clause . . . exhausts the mere fact of the idea; logically, there is nothing more to say. The additions stay with the same idea, probing its bearings and implications, exemplifying it or seeking an analogy or metaphor for it, or reducing it to details." Example: *"The fifteen-year-old dog stood unsteadily, fat and lumpy with age, the white whiskers shading her muzzle."*

basic rhetorical research. Research that investigates the exercise of rhetorical ability by observation of acts of speech or writing and that produces rhetorical theories that explain the rules to which utterances or written matter must conform if they are to be effective. Martin Steinmann, Jr., "Rhetorical Research," *New Rhetorics,* ed. Martin Steinmann, Jr. (New York: Charles Scribner's Sons, 1967), pp. 23-24.

basic writer. The student of writing who is restricted to a narrow range of syntactic, semantic, and rhetorical options, producing rudimentary or tangled prose with about fifteen to thirty-five errors per three hundred words, and who is characterized by nonacademic interests, pragmatic educational goals, and fear of failure in academic roles. Mina P. Shaughnessy, "Basic Writing," *Teaching Composition: 10 Bibliographical Essays,* ed. Gary Tate (Fort Worth: Texas Christian University Press, 1976), pp. 137-67. See also Mina P. Shaughnessy, *Error and Expectations* (New York: Oxford University Press, 1977).

black English vernacular (BEV). The dialect of a group of about 80 percent of black Americans of African ancestry that has structural and historical differences from the English spoken by most other Americans. For a study of its history and usage, see J. L. Dillard, *Black English* (New York: Random House, 1972).

blocs. See *discourse bloc* and *paragraph bloc.*

Bloom's taxonomy. From educational theory, a classification of educational goals and objectives which is intended to provide help for teachers, administrators, professional specialists, and research workers in dealing with curricular and evaluation problems. The objectives are classified as *cognitive* and *affective*. The *cognitive* group deals with the recall or recognition of knowledge and the development of intellectual abilities and skills. The *affective* group concerns changes in interests, attitudes, and values. Benjamin S. Bloom et al., eds., *Taxonomy of Educational Objectives* (New York: David McKay Co., 1956).

C

cant. The style of discourse characterized by the use and repetition of conventional, trite, or unexamined opinions.

cause and effect. One of the traditional topics of classical rhetoric that consists in arguing from the presence or absence of the cause to the existence or nonexistence of the effect or result; or, conversely, in arguing from an effect to its probable causes. Cause and effect can be an inventive procedure in which content is generated by looking for causes or effects in a particular situation. It can also be a method of organization for a piece of discourse or for a paragraph within. Lane Cooper, ed. and trans., *The Rhetoric of Aristotle* (New York: Appleton-Century-Crofts, 1932): "If you prove the cause, you at once prove the effect; and conversely nothing can exist without its cause." (p. 170) Example: "Here dead lie we because we did not choose / To live and shame the land from which we sprung."—A. E. Housman, from *More Poems.*

chains of meaning. See *equivalence chains.*

channel capacity. The limited amount of mental power available to the speaker or listener to recognize and to interpret symbols, to arrange and combine images, and to frame the thought expressed. For a discussion of its significance in composition see E. D. Hirsch, *The Philosophy of Composition* (Chicago: University of Chicago Press, 1977), p. 78.

claim. The conclusion or point of issue in an argument. Stephen Toulmin, *The Uses of Argument* (Cambridge: At the University Press, 1958). See also *data* and *warrant.*

classical rhetoric. The art of persuasion, descending chiefly from the rhetorics of Aristotle, Cicero, and Quintilian, and composed of five canons or arts—invention (*inventio*), arrangement (*dispositio*), style (*elocutio*), memory (*memoria*), and delivery (*pronuntiatio*). There were three occasions for the use of the art of persuasion: epideictic (for the present—i.e., during ceremonies, commemorative events, and arguments); deliberative (for the future); and judicial or forensic (judgments upon the past). Three means of persuasion were given: *ethos* (appeal based on the character of the speaker), *pathos* (appeal to the emotions of the audience), and *logos* (appeal through words or logical reason). For a complete discussion, see Edward P. J. Corbett, *Classical Rhetoric for the Modern Student* (New York: Oxford University Press, 1965; 2d ed., 1971). Lane Cooper's translation of *The Rhetoric of Aristotle* (New York: Appleton-Century-Crofts, 1932) presents a good introduction to the tradition.

classification. Usually with *division*. One of the traditional topics or ways of thinking about a subject that includes identifying the subject as part of a larger group with shared features. *Division* breaks the subject into smaller segments. For a discussion of classification as an underlying pattern of thought, see Frank J. D'Angelo, *A Conceptual Theory of Rhetoric* (Cambridge, Mass.: Winthrop Publishing Co., 1975), pp. 44-47. Example: "The fish belongs to the superclass Pisces, having fins, gills, and a streamlined body. This superclass includes the class Osteichthyes (having a bony skeleton), Chondrichthyes (having a cartilaginous skeleton), and Agnatha (lacking jaws)."

climax. A rhetorical figure in which parallel words or sentences build by degrees of increased weight. Example: "*Veni, vidi, vici.*" ("I came, I saw, I conquered.")—Julius Caesar.

code. The language or other communication signal that is common to the person speaking or writing (addresser) and the person listening or reading (addressee). Roman Jakobson, "Linguistics and Poetics," *Style in Language*, ed. Thomas A. Sebeok (New York: John Wiley & Sons and M.I.T. Press, 1960), pp. 350-77.

cognitive domain. The area of educational goals which has to do with the recall or recognition of knowledge and the development of intellectual abilities and skills. Benjamin S. Bloom et al., eds., *Taxonomy of Educational Objectives* (New York: David McKay Co., 1956). See *Bloom's taxonomy*.

communication triangle. The structure basic to all uses of language that includes a person who sends a message (see also *addresser* and *encoder*); the message itself, including the signal (*code* or language) which carries the message and the reality to which the message refers; and the receiver of the message (see also *addressee* and *decoder*). Aristotle made the triangle the basis of his *Rhetoric*. For a diagram, see James L. Kinneavy, *A Theory of Discourse* (Englewood Cliffs, N.J.: Prentice-Hall, 1971), p. 19.

communicative competence. Knowledge of language—in the sense of syntax, phonology, and semantics—and knowledge of the social world and its rules for using language so that speech is appropriate both linguistically and sociolinguistically and enables a speaker to communicate effectively to achieve self-identification and to conduct activities. For a definition, see Dell Hymes's preface to *Direction in Sociolinguistics,* ed. John H. Gumperz and Dell Hymes (New York: Holt, Rinehart & Winston, 1972). For further explanation, see Courtney B. Cazden, *Child Language and Education* (New York: Holt, Rinehart & Winston, 1972), p. 3.

communicative efficiency. The psycholinguistic principle of communication that determines that one piece of prose can be judged better than another because of its relative readability. E. D. Hirsch, *The Philosophy of Composition* (Chicago: University of Chicago Press, 1977), pp. 74-76:

> . . . the most efficient communication of *any* semantic intention, whether it be conformist or individualistic. Some semantic intentions require prose that is complex and difficult to read. An attempt to express those intentions in easy-to-read prose would properly be condemned as inefficient writing. (p. 75)

comparative rhetorical research. Research that investigates historically given theories of rhetoric and produces information about them and their relationships to one another. For example, such research might show how Kenneth Burke's and I. A. Richards's theories of rhetoric resemble and differ from one another and whether one theory seems to have influenced the other. Martin Steinmann, Jr., "Rhetorical Research," *New Rhetorics,* ed. Martin Steinmann, Jr. (New York: Charles Scribner's Sons, 1967), p. 26.

comparison. One of the traditional topics of rhetoric based on the assumption that a subject may be shown more clearly by pointing out ways it is similar to something else. The two subjects may each be explained separately and then their similarities pointed out, or they may be dealt with alternately point by point. See Leo Rockas, *Modes of Rhetoric* (New York: St. Martin's Press, 1964), pp. 60-61. Example: "parting day / Dies like the dolphin, whom each pang imbues / With a new colour as it gasps away, / The last still loveliest,—till—'tis gone—and all is gray."—Byron, *Childe Harold.* See also *contrast.*

competence. The potential ability to use the language that every native speaker of a language possesses by virtue of internalizing the system of rules that determine both the phonetic shape of the sentence and its intrinsic semantic content; knowledge of one's language as contrasted to one's performance with it. Noam Chomsky, appendix to Eric Lenneberg's *Biological Foundations of Language* (New York: John Wiley & Sons, 1967), reprinted in Chomsky's *Language and Mind* (New York: Harcourt Brace Jovanovich, 1972), pp. 115-60. See also *performance* and *communicative competence.*

complementation. A relationship of the parts of a discourse in which one part starts a unit of thought and a second part completes it. The term is used to describe such units of discourse in Willis Pitkin, Jr., "Discourse Blocs," *College Composition and Communication* 20 (May 1969), 138-48. Examples: question/answer, assertion/reassertion, cause/effect, negative/positive, premise/conclusion.

composing process. The activities that take place before and during the process of writing. In classical rhetoric these procedures were thought of as a discovery of the available means of persuasion in any rhetorical situation through the processes of invention (discovering the valid argument), arrangement, and style. In modern rhetoric the process is often thought of as including the following steps.

1. Prewriting. Finding a subject and determining what to say about the subject by gathering material from experience, research, and observation. For a discussion of this process, see D. Gordon Rohman, "Pre-Writing: The Stage of Discovery in the Writing Process," *College Composition and Communi-*

cation 16 (May 1965), 106-12; and Donald C. Stewart, *The Authentic Voice: A Pre-Writing Approach to Student Writing* (Dubuque, Iowa: William C. Brown, 1972).

2. Planning.

3. Revising.

Janet Emig has fully explored this process by case study in *The Composing Processes of Twelfth Graders,* Research Report No. 13 (Urbana, Ill.: NCTE, 1971). See also Charles R. Cooper and Lee Odell, eds., *Research on Composing: Points of Departure* (Urbana, Ill.: NCTE, 1978); and Frank J. D'Angelo, *A Conceptual Theory of Rhetoric* (Cambridge, Mass.: Winthrop Publishing Co., 1975), pp. 52-54.

conative function. The function of language in which the emphasis is upon bringing about a change in the person receiving the message. For a scheme of the functions, see Roman Jakobson, "Linguistics and Poetics," *Style in Language,* ed. Thomas A. Sebeok (New York: John Wiley & Sons and M.I.T. Press, 1960), pp. 350-77.

confirmatio. The fifth part of a traditional argument, consisting of the main body of the argument where the pros and cons are presented. See *argumentation.*

confutatio. The sixth part of a traditional argument, the part which refutes the opposing points of view. See *argumentation.*

connexity. A relationship between every pair of a collection. Morris R. Cohen and Ernest Nagel, *An Introduction to Logic and Scientific Method* (New York: Harcourt, Brace & World, 1934), pp. 113-16. For a discussion of its relation to rhetoric, see W. Ross Winterowd, *Rhetoric: A Synthesis* (New York: Holt, Rinehart & Winston, 1968), p. 144. For example, any number is either greater than or less than any other number; hence, either relation holds between any two numbers.

conscientization. The process by which men and women become aware of the social and cultural reality which shapes their lives and of their ability to transform that reality. Paulo Freire, "The Adult Literacy Process as Cultural Action for Freedom," trans. Loretta Stover, *Harvard Educational Review* 40 (May 1970), 205-25.

constative utterance. A straightforward statement of fact. J. L. Austin, *How to Do Things with Words* (Cambridge, Mass.: Harvard University Press, 1962), p. 3.

constraint. In information theory, a precise term for context that describes the reduction of possible alternatives in language use by increasing the probability of a few of them. E. D. Hirsch, *The Philosophy of Composition* (Chicago: University of Chicago Press, 1977), p. 102:

> *Constraint* is a precise, functional term for *context*. Everyone knows that we understand language with reference to its context, yet that vague formulation suggests nothing about the actual function of context in language processing. Its actual function is to impose constraints on the syntactic and semantic possibilities of speech. Because of the sequential character of language, these contextual constraints ought to be greater in the middle of a discourse than at the beginning. . . .

contact. The physical and psychological connection between the person speaking or writing (addresser) and the person addressed (addressee) that enables them to enter and to stay in communication. Roman Jakobson, "Linguistics and Poetics," *Style in Language,* ed. Thomas A. Sebeok (New York: John Wiley & Sons and M.I.T. Press, 1960), pp. 350-77.

content-oriented topic. In the process of invention, a topic or set of problem-solving probes in which the emphasis is on generating subject matter for speaking or writing. In a form-oriented topic, on the other hand, the emphasis is on providing a structure in which to place that subject matter. W. Ross Winterowd, "Invention," *Contemporary Rhetoric: A Conceptual Background with Readings* (New York: Harcourt Brace Jovanovich, 1975), pp. 43-45. For example, the traditional topics such as definition and cause and effect would be content-oriented because they encourage ways of thinking that create subject matter. See *form-oriented topic.*

contextual variation. The variation of the meaning of a word dependent on the entire context of the particular semantic occasion of its use. Because of this variation, particularly in expressive discourse and in poetry, terms cannot be controlled by explicit definition. Philip Wheelwright, *The Burning Fountain* (Bloomington: Indiana University Press, 1968), pp. 78-81.

contrast. One of the traditional topics of rhetoric based on the assumption that a subject may be shown more clearly by pointing out ways in which it is unlike another subject. See Leo Rockas, *Modes of Rhetoric* (New York: St. Martin's Press, 1964), pp. 60-61. Example: "If of Dryden's fire the blaze is brighter, of Pope's the heat is more regular and constant. Dryden often surpasses expectation, and Pope never falls below it. Dryden is read with frequent astonishment, and Pope with perpetual delight."–Samuel Johnson, *The Life of Pope.*

core. The main clause of a sentence expressed in simplest form. Example: "*She removed* the *keepsakes* from the shelves with exaggerated care."

correlation. In logic, a classification of the number of objects to which the referent may be connected by the relation: either *many-many* (Bob is the friend of Sam. Bob may have many other friends, and Sam may have many other friends); or *many-one* (Ted is the son of George. Others may stand in this relation to George, but only one may stand in this relation to Ted); or *one-many* (George is the father of Ted); or *one-one* (Five is greater by one than four). Morris R. Cohen and Ernest Nagel, *An Introduction to Logic and Scientific Method* (New York: Harcourt, Brace & Co., 1934), pp. 114-15. For a discussion of its use in rhetoric, see W. Ross Winterowd, *Rhetoric: A Synthesis* (New York: Holt, Rinehart & Winston, 1968), p. 144.

courtship. In rhetoric, overcoming social estrangement in a language situation and opening the lines of communication. Kenneth Burke, *A Rhetoric of Motives* (Berkeley: University of California Press, 1969), pp. 208-12. Example: "Hasn't the weather been hot lately?"

Crocean aesthetic monism. From Benedetto Croce, a theory of style that does not separate content and form; a work of art is a unified whole. For a discussion, see Louis T. Milic, "Theories of Style and Their Implications for the Teaching of Composition," *College Composition and Communication* 16 (May 1965), 67. See *dualism.*

crot. A bit or fragment used by a writer that works as an autonomous unit with an absence of transitional devices to preceding or subsequent units, thereby creating an effect of abruptness and rapid transition from one point of view to another. Crots are arranged in random or circular sequence, suggesting the fragmentation of contemporary experience. Winston Weathers, "Grammars of Style: New Options in Composition," *Freshman English News* 4 (Winter 1976), 4:

> The term was given new life by Tom Wolfe in his "Introduction" to a collection of *Esquire* magazine fiction, *The Secret Life of Our Times,* edited by Gordon Lish (New York: Doubleday, 1973). A basic element in the alternate grammar of style and comparable somewhat to the "stanza" in poetry, the crot may range in length from one sentence to twenty or thirty sentences.

Example: "Students and teacher in classroom (Drone of lecturer next door). Cold winter wind rattles leaves of trees outside window. Corn husks rattle in open field where rabbits hide and little boys take practice shots at rusty tin cans."

crucial issues.   See *issue.*

cumulative modifier.   See *free modifier* and *cumulative sentence.*

cumulative sentence.   A sentence in which the main clause, which may or may not have a sentence modifier before it, advances the discussion, and in which the additions modify the statement of the main clause, staying with the same idea, probing its implications, exemplifying it, creating an analogy or metaphor for it, or adding details to it. The main clause is likely to be at a high level of generality. By this method of writing sentences, writers are said to "generate" ideas. Francis Christensen, "A Generative Rhetoric of the Sentence," *College Composition and Communication* 14 (October 1963), 155-61. Example: "He shook his hands, a quick shake, fingers down, like a pianist."—Sinclair Lewis. See *generative rhetoric.*

D

data.   Evidence for the claim in an argument. Stephen Toulmin, *The Uses of Argument* (Cambridge: At the University Press, 1958). See also *claim* and *warrant.*

decoder.   In communication theory, the audience or receiver of the message. Used in the communication triangle of James L. Kinneavy, *A Theory of Discourse* (Englewood Cliffs, N.J.: Prentice-Hall, 1971), p. 19: "Basic to all uses of language are a person who encodes a message, the signal (language) which carries the message, the reality to which the message refers, and the decoder (receiver of the message)."

definition. One of the traditional topics or patterns of thought which places a subject into an appropriate class and then differentiates the subject from the other members of that class. The first step limits the meaning of the subject; the second step specifies its meaning. In prose, definitions are often extended by illustrations and examples. See Leo Rockas, *Modes of Rhetoric* (New York: St. Martin's Press, 1964), pp. 55-78. One of the best and most recent discussions of definition is in Ann E. Berthoff, *Forming, Thinking, Writing: The Composing Imagination* (Rochelle Park, N.J.: Hayden Book Co., 1978), pp. 94-104. See also Frank J. D'Angelo, *A Conceptual Theory of Rhetoric* (Cambridge, Mass.: Winthrop Publishing Co., 1975), pp. 44-47.

delayed-completion topic sentence. A topic of a paragraph stated in two separate units of thought, not necessarily adjacent. Richard Braddock, "The Frequency and Placement of Topic Sentences in Expository Prose," *Research in the Teaching of English* 8 (Winter 1974), 287-302. See *topic sentence.*

deliberative discourse. That kind of discourse which recommends a course of action or urges an audience to refrain from a course of action in the future. In Aristotle's *Rhetoric,* speeches of counsel or advice, such as political speeches, proposals for legislation, appeals to end wars. Lane Cooper, ed. and trans., *The Rhetoric of Aristotle* (New York: Appleton-Century-Crofts, 1932), p. 17: "The elements of deliberation [counsel] are (a) exhortation [encouragement], (b) dissuasion; for, as advice given in private always has one or the other aspect, so is it with those who discuss matters of State in public—they either exhort or dissuade."

description. The traditional classification of discourse that pictures images verbally in space and time and arranges those images in a logical pattern, such as spatial, or according to association. The traditional modes of discourse—narration, description, argumentation, and exposition—are believed to have been first identified as such by Alexander Bain in *English Composition and Rhetoric* (American edition, New York: D. Appleton & Co., 1890). See Frank J. D'Angelo, "Modes of Discourse," *Teaching Composition: 10 Bibliographical Essays,* ed. Gary Tate

(Fort Worth: Texas Christian University Press, 1976), p. 115. For a recent discussion of description as an underlying pattern of thought, see D'Angelo, *A Conceptual Theory of Rhetoric* (Cambridge, Mass.: Winthrop Publishing Co., 1975), pp. 44-47.

devil term. A term so repulsive that it stands at the opposite end of the spectrum from *god term.* Richard M. Weaver, *The Ethics of Rhetoric* (Chicago: Henry Regnery Co., 1953), p. 222. Example: "un-American."

diachronic stylistics. The study of changes in national literary style from one period to the next. Although at any period there are many different styles of writing, this study looks for signs of similarities in prose style which seem to dominate in a particular historical period ("synchronic stylistics") and compares those characteristics with the characteristics of the preceding or following period. See Richard Ohmann, "Generative Grammars and the Concept of Literary Style," *New Rhetorics,* ed. Martin Steinmann, Jr. (New York: Charles Scribner's Sons, 1967), p. 136. See also *synchronic stylistics.*

dialectal varieties. A term used in linguistics to denote the linguistic reflection of reasonably permanent characteristics of a person in a language situation, as delimited by individual, temporal, geographical, and social distinctions—constant features in language situations. Michael Gregory, "Aspects of Varieties Differentiation," *Journal of Linguistics* 3 (October 1967), 177-98. Examples: Mr. X's English, Miss Y's English, Old English, Modern English, British English, American English, upper class English, middle class English, standard English, nonstandard English.

diatypic varieties. The recurrent linguistic characteristics of a person's *use* of language in situations, governed by that person's role, relationship to audience, and the discourse requirements. Michael Gregory, "Aspects of Varieties Differentiation," *Journal of Linguistics* 3 (October 1967), 177-98. Examples: technical English, nontechnical English, spoken English, written English, formal English, informal English, didactic English, nondidactic English.

digressio. The seventh part of the traditional argument in which an illustration, a parallel, or a useful point to support the argument is introduced. See *argumentation.*

direction of modification. The direction, either before or after, in which modifiers are added to the noun, verb, or main clause of a sentence, or to the thesis or lead sentence of a paragraph. Francis Christensen, "A Generative Rhetoric of the Sentence," *College Composition and Communication* 14 (October 1963), 155-61; reprinted in Francis Christensen and Bonniejean Christensen, *Notes Toward a New Rhetoric*, 2d ed. (New York: Harper & Row, 1978), pp. 26-27:

> But speech is linear, moving in time, and writing moves in linear space, which is analogous to time. When you add a modifier, whether to the noun, the verb, or the main clause, you must add it either before the head or after it. If you add it before the head, the direction of modification can be indicated by an arrow pointing forward; if you add it after, by an arrow pointing backward.

discourse. Verbal expression in speech or writing; a coherent and reasoned treatment of a subject; a lengthy treatment of a subject; a conversation. James Moffett, *Teaching the Universe of Discourse* (Boston: Houghton Mifflin Co., 1968), pp. 10-11: "any piece of verbalization complete for its original purpose." James L. Kinneavy, *A Theory of Discourse* (Englewood Cliffs, N.J.: Prentice-Hall, 1971), p. 4:

> . . . the full text (when feasible) of an oral or written situation; it does not denote necessarily a rational or logically coherent content; the discourse can be directed to any aim of language or refer to any kind of reality; it can be a poem, a conversation, a tragedy, a joke, a seminar discussion, a full-length history, a periodical article, an interview, a sermon, a TV ad.

discourse bloc. In a discourse, a unit of thought which is arranged hierarchically with other units according to the functions they serve in the discourse. A bloc may be several sentences or paragraphs or a part of a single sentence. Willis Pitkin, Jr., "Discourse Blocs," *College Composition and Communication* 20 (May 1969), 138-48.

dispositio. Also *arrangement.* The second of the five traditional canons or parts of rhetoric, having to do with ordering a discourse. See *form.*

division. See *classification.*

doublespeak. A type of evasive language, often marked by an absence of specific authorship, in which the speaker or writer

obscures the ideas and in which the generalizations and abstrac-
tions are rarely supported by concrete details. Political speeches,
advertising, and government reports are often the source of
doublespeak. For a working definition, see Terence P. Moran,
"Public Doublespeak: On Communication and Pseudocommuni-
cation," *College English* 36 (September 1974), 112-18. The
NCTE Committee on Public Doublespeak has produced the following publications: Hugh Rank, ed., *Language and Public
Policy* (Urbana, Ill.: NCTE, 1974); Daniel Dieterich, ed.,
Teaching about Doublespeak (Urbana, Ill.: NCTE, 1976). Example: "a crescendo of military moves against infiltration tar-
gets"—*The Pentagon Papers.*

downplay. The second part of the intensify/downplay schema
for teaching basic patterns of persuasion used in political propaganda and in commercial advertising. Downplay is accomplished
by three means: omission, the deliberate concealing or hiding
of information; diversion, the distracting of the reader from key
issues or important items; and confusion, the deliberate inclusion of complications and complexities so that people "give up."
Hugh Rank, "Intensify/Downplay," *College English* 39 (September 1977), 109-11. See also *intensify.*

dramatic *ethos*. Fictional creations of *ethos* in literature, public
service advertisements, etc., in which an image of virtue is created for the character. Jim W. Corder, "Varieties of Ethical Argument, with Some Account of the Significance of *Ethos* in
the Teaching of Composition," *Freshman English News* 6 (Winter 1978), 14.

dramatistic framework. Or *dramatistic method.* A set of five
problem-solving probes answering the following questions concerning a thought or event: What was done (act)? When and
where was it done (scene)? Who did it (agent)? How was it done
(agency)? and Why was it done (purpose)? Kenneth Burke, *A
Grammar of Motives* (New York: Prentice-Hall, 1945). See
Pentad.

dualism. Also *rhetorical dualism.* The theory of style, originating
in classical times, which says that ideas exist separately from
style and can be presented in a variety of styles—grand, plain,
middle, low, etc.—depending upon the occasion. Louis T. Milic,
"Theories of Style and Their Implications for the Teaching of
Composition," *College Composition and Communication* 16
(May 1965), 67. See *Crocean aesthetic monism.*

dyadic argument. An argumentative situation in which the speaker or writer directs the message to the audience he or she seeks to change. Richard E. Young, Alton L. Becker, and Kenneth L. Pike, *Rhetoric: Discovery and Change* (New York: Harcourt, Brace & World, 1970), p. 273. See also *triadic argument.*

E

efficient *ethos.* The ability of a speaker or writer to meet all the demands of a particular and limited rhetorical situation but not to expand to the structural and stylistic demands of a new rhetorical situation. Certain folk heroes and archetypal figures, such as Robin Hood and Beowulf, have this form of *ethos.* Jim W. Corder, "Varieties of Ethical Argument, with Some Account of the Significance of *Ethos* in the Teaching of Composition," *Freshman English News* 6 (Winter 1978), 14.

egocentric speech. An early speech habit of monologue and running commentary that makes no attempt to see the world from another person's point of view. Jean Piaget, *The Language and Thought of the Child,* trans. Marjorie Gabain, 3d ed. (New York: Humanities Press, 1959), p. 35:

> Ego-centric language is, as we have seen, the group made up by the first three of the categories we have enumerated—repetition, monologue, and collective monologue. All three have this in common, that they consist of remarks that are not addressed to anyone, or not to anyone in particular, and that they evoke no reaction adapted to them on the part of anyone to whom they may chance to be addressed.

ejaculative discourse. The mode of discourse characterized by strong feeling or emotion. Philip Wheelwright, *The Burning Fountain* (Bloomington: Indiana University Press, 1968), pp. 58-68. Example: "Damn it!"

elaborated code. Speech forms which are not restricted to a provincial structure and which make it possible for the users to be understood out of their own geographical, social, and cultural environments; for example, the users of standard English have more social and cultural mobility than the users of a localized dialect. Basil Bernstein, "Language, Socialization and Subcultures," *Language and Social Context,* ed. Pier Paolo Giglioli (Baltimore: Penguin Books, 1972), pp. 163-64. See *restricted code.*

elocutio. The third of the five traditional canons or parts of rhetoric that refers to the style of discourse. See *style*.

emotional argument. See *pathos*.

emotive function. The function of language that is focused on the speaker or writer and aims at direct expression of that person's attitude toward what he or she is speaking or writing about. Attributing the term to A. Marty, Roman Jakobson uses *emotive* as one of the functions of language in "Linguistics and Poetics," *Style in Language,* ed. Thomas A. Sebeok (New York: John Wiley & Sons and M.I.T. Press, 1960), pp. 350-77.

enactive representation. In learning theory, the transferring of experiences into a mental model of the world through the learning of behavioral responses and forms of action, such as in learning to play tennis or to ski. Jerome S. Bruner, *Toward a Theory of Instruction* (Cambridge, Mass.: Harvard University Press, Belknap Press, 1966), p. 11.

encoder. In communication theory, the speaker or writer of discourse. Used in the communication triangle of James L. Kinneavy in *A Theory of Discourse* (Englewood Cliffs, N.J.: Prentice-Hall, 1971), p. 19.

Engfish. Pretentious language that says nothing and is devoid of the rhythms of contemporary speech. Ken Macrorie, *Uptaught* (New York: Hayden Book Co., 1971). Example: "The youth of today need to become aware that tradition is hard to break. Times are changing, the ways of the modern world are different, and the contributions of our older generations cannot be denied."

enthymeme. A term used by Aristotle in the *Rhetoric* to mean a syllogism in which the premises are only generally true; today it has come to mean a shortened syllogism of any sort. Lane Cooper, ed. and trans., *The Rhetoric of Aristotle* (New York: Appleton-Century-Crofts, 1932), p. 5:

> The enthymeme, again, is a kind of syllogism; now every kind of syllogism falls within the province of Dialectic, and must be examined under Dialectic as a whole, or under some branch of it. Consequently the person with the clearest insight into the nature of syllogisms, who knows from what premises and in what modes they may be constructed, will also be the most expert in

regard to enthymemes, once he has mastered their special province [of things contingent and uncertain such as human actions and their consequences], and has learnt the differences between enthymemes and logical syllogisms. [The latter are complete, and yield an absolute demonstration.]

In the introduction to the *Rhetoric*, Lane Cooper says of the enthymeme:

But, again, an enthymeme may be a maxim of one term; so Lincoln's "All men are created equal." Or, again, it may be a maxim of two terms, yet not syllogistic; such are all the Beatitudes: "Blessed are the pure in heart, for they shall see God." The arguments good speakers actually use in persuasion are enthymemes. (p. xxvi)

For a description of the enthymeme in modern rhetoric, see Earl W. Wiley, "The Enthymeme: Idiom of Persuasion," *Quarterly Journal of Speech* 42 (February 1956), 19-24:

Such precision in reasoning we leave to the needs of demonstration. An enthymeme, on the other hand, is one man's judgment of the propriety of events in some conflict involving people; being contingent, it is not demonstration, and being controversial, it is framed in argument. Patterns of the frame are various, and these are designated by Aristotle as topics. (p. 19)

epideictic discourse. The kind of discourse for an occasion, sometimes called *ceremonial;* discourse of the present. Lane Cooper, ed. and trans., *The Rhetoric of Aristotle* (New York: Appleton-Century-Crofts, 1932), p. 17. Examples: commemorative addresses and speeches of censure or praise.

equivalence chains. Chains of words and phrases within the sentences of discourse that occur in the environment of other identical or almost identical elements. Zellig S. Harris, "Discourse Analysis," *Language* 28 (1952), 1-30; reprinted in *The Structure of Language*, ed. Jerry A. Fodor and Jerrold J. Katz (Englewood Cliffs, N.J.: Prentice-Hall, 1964), pp. 355-83:

Suppose our text contains the following four sentences: *The trees turn here about the middle of autumn; The trees turn here about the end of October; The first frost comes after the middle of autumn; We start heating after the end of October.* Then we may say that *the middle of autumn* and *the end of October* are equivalent because they occur in the same environment (*The trees turn here about*—), and that this equivalence is carried over into the latter two sentences. (p. 360)

Using *equivalence chains* to refer to words and phrases having the same referent, W. Ross Winterowd illustrates how equivalence chains give a paragraph coherence in *The Contemporary Writer* (New York: Harcourt Brace Jovanovich, 1975), p. 114. Example:

> An interesting stylistic feature of the painting is the use of *a light source. The sun,* or *light bulb,* or *eye* at the top of the painting radiates planes of light which provide the triangular structure. *This source of light* is reminiscent of Goya's use of *a light source* in "The Third of May," where the same triangular effect is accomplished.

eristic dialogue. A dialogue in which one participant aims at overpowering the other. Chaim Perelman and L. Olbrechts-Tyteca, *The New Rhetoric,* trans. John Wilkinson and Purcell Weaver (Notre Dame, Ind.: University of Notre Dame Press, 1969), p. 37. See also *heuristic dialogue.*

ethos. Also *ethical argument.* An appeal based on the character of the speaker; one of three means of persuasion: *logos, pathos,* and *ethos.* Lane Cooper, ed. and trans., *The Rhetoric of Aristotle* (New York: Appleton-Century-Crofts, 1932), p. 8:

> The character [*ethos*] of the speaker is a cause of persuasion when the speech is so uttered as to make him worthy of belief; for as a rule we trust men of probity more, and more quickly, about things in general, while on points outside the realm of exact knowledge, where opinion is divided, we trust them absolutely.

For a recent analysis of *ethos,* see Otis M. Walter, "Toward an Analysis of *Ethos,*" *Pennsylvania Speech Annual* 21 (1964), 37:

> *Ethos* arises only when there is a strong need, only when the need can best be gratified by another, and only when such needs are perceived to be (correctly or incorrectly) worthy.

See also Richard M. Weaver, *The Ethics of Rhetoric* (Chicago: Henry Regnery Co., 1953). Jim W. Corder, in "Varieties of Ethical Argument, with Some Account of the Significance of *Ethos* in the Teaching of Composition," *Freshman English News* 6 (Winter 1978), has identified the forms of *ethos:* dramatic, gratifying, functional, efficient, and generative. See each of these and *rhetorical situation.*

exchange-value. The aspect of a message which indicates how the person receiving it should relate to the message and to the person sending it. Richard M. Coe, "The Rhetoric of Paradox,"

A Symposium in Rhetoric, ed. William E. Tanner, J. Dean Bishop, and Turner S. Kobler (Denton: Texas Woman's University Press, 1976), p. 6. Example: In asking, "How are you?" the *truth-value* of the reply may not be as important as the relationship established. See also *truth-value.*

existential sentence. From logic, traditionally a sentence which directly asserts the existence of its subject by the use of the copulative verb: "There is . . ."; "There are. . . ." As an inventive technique, the existential sentence (x is y) can be used to link an abstraction to a concrete observation, thus translating a generalization to one's own experience. See Donald C. Stewart, *The Authentic Voice: A Pre-Writing Approach to Student Writing* (Dubuque, Iowa: William C. Brown, 1972). Example: "Love is coming home from work and finding your spouse preparing dinner."

exordium. In traditional argument, the opening in which a writer or speaker attracts the audience's attention, establishes his or her reliability, and creates a sense of good intentions. These purposes are often accomplished by an anecdote or illustration. See *argumentation.*

exploratory discourse. A classification of discourse concerned with the process of finding and discovering probabilities. Historically, "dialectic," "discovery," "inquiry," "heuristic," and "essay" have been used synonymously for this kind of discourse. James L. Kinneavy, *A Theory of Discourse* (Englewood Cliffs, N.J.: Prentice-Hall, 1971), pp. 96-106. Examples: dialogues, seminars, diagnoses, tentative definitions.

exposition. One of the traditional classifications of discourse that has as a function to inform or to instruct or to present ideas and general truths objectively. Exposition uses all of the common organizational patterns such as definition, analysis, classification, cause and effect, etc. Alexander Bain is believed to have been the first to identify this as a mode of discourse in *English Composition and Rhetoric* (American edition, New York: D. Appleton & Co., 1890).

expressive discourse. Discourse in which the personal stake of the speaker in the discourse is the most dominant feature, as in the classical distinction of poetic from rhetoric. Expressive discourse is identified as a mode of discourse in Philip Wheelwright's *The Burning Fountain* (Bloomington: Indiana University Press, 1968), pp. 69-70. James L. Kinneavy, in *A Theory of Discourse* (Englewood Cliffs, N.J.: Prentice-Hall, 1971), pp. 393-449, also uses *expressive* as a classification of discourse and gives the following examples: individual—diaries, journals, conversations, prayers; social—minority protests, manifestos, declarations of independence, religious credos.

extensive writing. The mode of writing that focuses upon sending a message or communicating with another. Janet Emig, *The Composing Processes of Twelfth Graders*, Research Report No. 13 (Urbana, Ill.: NCTE, 1971), p. 4: "the domain explored is usually the cognitive; the style is assured, impersonal, and often reportorial." See also *reflexive writing*.

extrinsic proof. Means of persuasion other than the art of speech. Also called *inartistic proof* or *non-artistic proof*. Aristotle in the *Rhetoric* lists torture, oaths, laws, witnesses, and contracts. Brainwashing would be a form of extrinsic proof.

F

field. One of the three perspectives of tagmemic invention that views data as orderly systems of relationships. Kenneth L. Pike, "Language as Particle, Wave, and Field," *Texas Quarterly* 2 (Summer 1959), 37-54. See also Richard E. Young and Alton L. Becker, "Toward a Modern Theory of Rhetoric: A Tagmemic Contribution," *Harvard Educational Review* 35 (Fall 1965), 450-68. For elaboration of the tagmemic contribution to composition, see Young, Becker, and Pike, *Rhetoric: Discovery and Change* (New York: Harcourt, Brace & World, 1970). For example, a *field* description of a plant would partition the plant into its parts or would place the plant into a classification of other similar plants in a taxonomical system. See also *particle, wave,* and *tagmemic invention*.

figurative term. In a metaphor, the thing to which the literal term, or the thing being discussed, is compared. Laurence Perrine, "Four Forms of Metaphor," *College English* 33 (November 1971), 125-38. Example: "Wit is the *salt* of conversation, not the food."—Hazlitt. See also *literal term*.

finite topics. A list of topics or set of questions that does not allow for any additional topics or questions. W. Ross Winterowd,

"Invention," *Contemporary Rhetoric: A Conceptual Background with Readings* (New York: Harcourt Brace Jovanovich, 1975), pp. 41-42. Example: Burke's Pentad.

forensic discourse. Also called *judicial discourse.* The kind of discourse that concerns the justice or injustice of a past action. Lane Cooper, ed. and trans., *The Rhetoric of Aristotle* (New York: Appleton-Century-Crofts, 1932), p. 17: "to the judicial pleader belongs the past, for it is always with regard to things already done that the one party accuses and the other defends." Example: the discourse of law courts.

form. The structure of the complete piece of discourse or of its identifiable parts. *Form* is often used in modern rhetoric as a synonym for what was called *dispositio,* organization, or arrangement in traditional rhetoric. For a good discussion of form in traditional rhetoric, see Edward P. J. Corbett, *Classical Rhetoric for the Modern Student,* 2d ed. (New York: Oxford University Press, 1971), chap. 3. More recent definitions of *form* include the following:

a. "the internal set of consistent relationships perceived in any stretch of discourse, whether poem, play, essay, oration, or whatever. . . ." W. Ross Winterowd, *"Dispositio:* The Concept of Form in Discourse," *College Composition and Communication* 22 (February 1971), 41.

b. "comprises those elements in an expression that reflect the attitude of the speaker and that tend to control the audience's relation to the expression's subject matter and the speaker. . . ." Keith Fort, "Form, Authority, and the Critical Essay," *College English* 32 (March 1971), 629-39.

c. "an arousing and fulfillment of desires. . . ." Kenneth Burke, "The Nature of Form," from *Counter-Statement,* available in *Contemporary Rhetoric: A Conceptual Background with Readings,* ed. W. Ross Winterowd (New York: Harcourt Brace Jovanovich, 1975), pp. 183-99.

The essays quoted in the first two examples may also be found in Winterowd's book.

form-oriented topic. A topic or set of problem-solving probes that produces writing fitting a predetermined organizational structure. By contrast, a content-oriented topic produces subject matter. W. Ross Winterowd, "Invention," *Contemporary*

Rhetoric: A Conceptual Background with Readings (New York: Harcourt Brace Jovanovich, 1975), pp. 43-45. Example: Alton L. Becker's T-R-I (topic, restriction, illustration). See *content-oriented topic.*

free modifier. A sentence modifier such as a nonrestrictive relative or subordinate clause or a noun, verb, or adjective cluster which is added to the main or base clause of a sentence in the initial, medial, or final position. Francis Christensen and Bonniejean Christensen, *Notes Toward a New Rhetoric,* 2d ed. (New York: Harper & Row, 1978), p. 29. W. Ross Winterowd calls them *cumulative modifiers* because they create the cumulative sentence. See *The Contemporary Writer* (New York: Harcourt Brace Jovanovich, 1975), p. 363.

functional *ethos*. The form of *ethos* that creates a mark of recognition for the speaker of the discourse. Jim W. Corder, "Varieties of Ethical Argument, with Some Account of the Significance of *Ethos* in the Teaching of Composition," *Freshman English News* 6 (Winter 1978), 14. Example: the *ethos* of advertising and brand names.

G

generative *ethos*. A progressive form of ethical quality that is in the process of making itself and of liberating its hearers. Jim W. Corder, "Varieties of Ethical Argument, with Some Account of the Significance of *Ethos* in the Teaching of Composition," *Freshman English News* 6 (Winter 1978), 14. Example: the *ethos* of the Gettysburg Address.

generative rhetoric. A collection of procedures for initiating, encouraging, and generating discourse; advice about the composing process. See Robert M. Gorrell, "In Pursuit of a Generative Rhetoric," *Rhetoric Society Quarterly* 7 (Winter 1977), 20-25. In the sense of Francis Christensen's *generative rhetoric,* the term is a procedure for producing ideas based on the concept that composition is essentially a process of addition. Francis Christensen, "A Generative Rhetoric of the Sentence," *College Composition and Communication* 14 (October 1963), 155-61; and "A Generative Rhetoric of the Paragraph," *College Composition and Communication* 16 (October 1965), 144-56. See *cumulative sentence.*

gobbledygook. Language that is wordy and bombastic. Coined by Maury Maverick, a Congressman from Texas, and quoted in Stuart Chase's *Power of Words* (New York: Harcourt Brace Jovanovich, 1954), p. 249. Chase defines *gobbledygook* as "using two, or three, or ten words in the place of one, or using a five-syllable word where a single syllable would suffice."

god term. The expression beneath which all other expressions are ranked as subordinate and whose force fixes the scale according to which all other terms can be ranked. Kenneth Burke, *A Grammar of Motives* (New York: Prentice-Hall, 1945), pp. 106-13. Richard M. Weaver, *The Ethics of Rhetoric* (Chicago: Henry Regnery Co., 1953), p. 212. Examples: "progress," "money."

good reasons. From ethics, a number of statements consistent with each other, offered in support of an *ought* proposition or of a value judgment. Karl R. Wallace, "The Substance of Rhetoric: Good Reasons," *Quarterly Journal of Speech* 49 (October 1963), 239-49.

grammar of coherence. A grammar of form involving a set of consistent relationships beyond case and syntax called *transitions.* There are seven of these relationships:

1. coordinate, expressed by *and* or its synonyms: *furthermore, in addition, too, also, again;*
2. observative, expressed by *but* or its synonyms: *yet, however, on the other hand;*
3. causative, expressed by *for;*
4. conclusive, expressed by *so* or its synonyms: *therefore, thus, for this reason;*
5. alternative, expressed by *or;*
6. inclusive, expressed often by a colon or the relationship of an example to a generality;
7. sequential, expressed by "first—second—third," "earlier—later," etc.

W. Ross Winterowd, "The Grammar of Coherence," *College English* 31 (May 1970), 828-35. Reprinted in *Contemporary Rhetoric: A Conceptual Background with Readings,* ed. W. Ross Winterowd (New York: Harcourt Brace Jovanovich, 1975), pp. 225-33.

grammar of style. The set of conventions that governs the construction of a composition; the criteria that a writer uses to select the stylistic materials, method of organization, and pattern or structure to prepare a particular composition. Winston Weathers, "Grammars of Style: New Options in Composition," *Freshman English News* 4 (Winter 1976), 2: "This 'grammar' defines and establishes the boundaries in which a composition must take place and defines the communication goals to which a composition is committed."

grapholect. A national *written* language distinguished historically and structurally from any dialect. It is edited (freed of the erroneous utterances and false starts of the speaker), analyzed (separated into sequential units, phonemes, and words), delayed (learned as a second language with greater reflection and elaboration than that used to learn to speak), and stabilized (can be stored). Einar Haugen, "Linguistics and Language Planning," *Sociolinguistics,* ed. W. Bright (The Hague: Mouton Publishers, 1966), pp. 50-71.

gratifying *ethos*. The quality of a speaker that fulfills a need of the hearer which the hearer judges to be a worthy need. Jim W. Corder, "Varieties of Ethical Argument, with Some Account of the Significance of *Ethos* in the Teaching of Composition," *Freshman English News* 6 (Winter 1978), 14. Example: the *ethos* of television entertainers.

H

headword. The word, usually a noun, in a piece of descriptive writing to which descriptive detail concerning qualities or attributes is added. Francis Christensen, "A Lesson from Hemingway," *College English* (October 1963), 12-18; reprinted in Francis Christensen and Bonniejean Christensen, *Notes Toward a New Rhetoric,* 2d ed. (New York: Harper & Row, 1978), pp. 45-60. Example: "the *hickories* with their buds almost like flowers."

heuristic. (noun) A method of solving problems; a series of steps or questions which are likely to lead to a solution of a problem. There are two kinds of heuristics: a taxonomy of the sorts of solutions that have been found in the past; and an epistemological heuristic, a method of inquiry based on assumptions about how something comes to be known. Some examples of recent heuristics are Burke's Pentad and Young, Becker, and Pike's particle, wave, and field. For a good discussion of heuristic procedures, see Richard E. Young, "Invention: A Topographical Survey," *Teaching Composition: 10 Bibliographical Essays,* ed. Gary Tate (Fort Worth: Texas Christian University Press, 1976), pp. 1-43, where he defines *heuristic* as "specific plans for analyzing and searching which focus attention, guide reason, stimulate memory and encourage intuition." (p. 1)

heuristic dialogue. A dialogue in which the participants search honestly and without bias for the best solution or answer to a problem. Chaim Perelman and L. Olbrechts-Tyteca, *The New Rhetoric,* trans. John Wilkinson and Purcell Weaver (Notre Dame, Ind.: University of Notre Dame Press, 1969), p. 37:

> Dialogue, as we consider it, is not supposed to be a *debate,* in which the partisans of opposed settled convictions defend their respective views, but rather a *discussion,* in which the interlocutors search honestly and without bias for the best solution to a controversial problem. Certain contemporary writers who stress this heuristic viewpoint, as against the eristic one, hold that discussion is the ideal instrument for reaching objectively valid conclusions.

See also *eristic dialogue.*

historical rhetorical research. Research that investigates historically given theories of rhetoric and produces information about them and their historical or comparative relationships. Martin Steinmann, Jr., "Rhetorical Research," *New Rhetorics,* ed. Martin Steinmann, Jr. (New York: Charles Scribner's Sons, 1967), p. 26.

hyperbole. A rhetorical figure composed of exaggerated words or ideas used for emphasis or effect and not to be taken literally. Example: "An apple a day keeps the doctor away."

I

iconic representation. In learning theory, the transferring of experiences into a mental model of the world through visual or sensory organization or the use of summarizing images, that is, through the perceptions. Jerome S. Bruner, *Toward a Theory of Instruction* (Cambridge, Mass.: Harvard University Press,

Belknap Press, 1966), p. 10-11, 13: "If at first 'a rattle is to shake' and 'a hole is to dig,' later they are somehow picturable or conceivable without action." (p. 13)

ideational function. The use of language for the expression of content. Through this function speakers or writers embody their experiences of the real world including the world of their own consciousness—their reactions, perceptions, and linguistic acts of speaking and understanding. The ideational function also involves expression of logical relations such as coordination, apposition, modification, and the like. M. A. K. Halliday, *Explorations in the Functions of Language* (New York: Elsevier–North Holland Publishing Co., 1977), pp. 29ff, 97-98. See also M. A. K. Halliday, *Learning How to Mean* (London: Edward Arnold, 1975), pp. 17ff. See also *interpersonal function* and *textual function.*

identification. The process of identifying one's ways with another while retaining one's own identity, and thus understanding another in his or her dramatistic role. Kenneth Burke, "Rhetoric—Old and New," *Journal of General Education* 5 (April 1951), 202-9. See also Burke's *A Rhetoric of Motives* (Berkeley: University of California Press, 1969), pp. 19ff, 55ff: "You persuade a man only insofar as you can talk his language by speech, gesture, tonality, order, image, attitude, idea, *identifying* your ways with his." (p. 55) See also *dramatistic framework.*

illocutionary act. The act performed by a speaker or writer in saying something; for example, informing, ordering, warning, stating. J. L. Austin, *How to Do Things with Words* (Cambridge, Mass.: Harvard University Press, 1962), p. 98:

> To determine what illocutionary act is so performed we must determine in what way we are using the locution: asking or answering a question, giving some information or an assurance or a warning, announcing a verdict or an intention, pronouncing sentence, making an appointment or an appeal or a criticism, making an identification or giving a description, and the numerous like.

See also John R. Searle, *Speech Acts* (Cambridge: At the University Press, 1969), pp. 54-71. See *speech act theory.*

implied audience. The audience imagined by a writer before composition; the writer predicts this audience's probable response to and understanding and imagined projection of himself or herself. Chaim Perelman and L. Olbrechts-Tyteca, *Rhétorique et philoso-*

phie (Paris: Presses Universitaires de France, 1952), pp. 20-22. Expanded in E. D. Hirsch, *The Philosophy of Composition* (Chicago: University of Chicago Press, 1977), pp. 27-28.

impressionism. Regarding style in rhetoric, the application of metaphorical labels to styles, such as "masculine," "staccato," "flowing," etc.; and the attempt to evaluate styles in these terms. Richard Ohmann, "Generative Grammars and the Concept of Literary Style," *New Rhetorics,* ed. Martin Steinmann, Jr. (New York: Charles Scribner's Sons, 1967), p. 136.

inartistic proof. See *extrinsic proof.*

individualist monism. A theory of style as the dynamic expression of a writer's personality. Having as its origin perhaps Plato, it has its modern roots in Montaigne. Louis T. Milic, "Theories of Style and Their Implications for the Teaching of Composition," *College Composition and Communication* 16 (May 1965), 67.

inferred topic sentence. A topic not stated by the writer but construed by the reader from several sentences of a paragraph. Richard Braddock, "The Frequency and Placement of Topic Sentences in Expository Prose," *Research in the Teaching of English* 8 (Winter 1974), 287-302. See *topic sentence.*

informative discourse. Discourse that focuses on providing the receiver with information. An informative statement is measured by its factuality, its comprehensiveness, and the degree of predictability of the information given. Three kinds of information have been distinguished by James L. Kinneavy: syntactic (the words or word-strings), semantic (what and how much information about reality the discourse gives), and pragmatic (the relevance of the information to the listener or reader). For a complete discussion, see James L. Kinneavy, *A Theory of Discourse* (Englewood Cliffs, N.J.: Prentice-Hall, 1971), pp. 89-96. Examples: news articles, reports, summaries, textbooks, nontechnical encyclopedia articles. See also *pragmatic information, semantic information,* and *syntactic information.*

intensify. The first part of the intensify/downplay schema for teaching basic patterns of persuasion used in political propaganda and commercial advertising. Intensification is accomplished by repetition, association or linking, and composition (pattern and arrangement using design, variations in sequence, and variations in proportion that add to the force of words, images, and movements). Hugh Rank, "Intensify/Downplay," *College English* 39 (September 1977), 109-11. See also *downplay*.

interinanimation. The idea that words are mutually dependent upon one another for their meanings and that no word can be judged good or bad, correct or incorrect, or anything else, in isolation. I. A. Richards, *The Philosophy of Rhetoric* (New York: Oxford University Press, 1965), pp. 47-66: "the effects on words of their combination in sentences, and how their meaning depends upon the other words before and after them in the sentence." (p. 47)

interlocutor.   A participant in a dialogue or conversation.

interpersonal function.   The use of language in the establishment and maintenance of human relationships; the expression of comments, attitudes, and evaluations and the expression of the relationship between the speaker and the listener. M. A. K. Halliday, *Explorations in the Functions of Language* (New York: Elsevier–North Holland Publishing Co., 1977), pp. 33ff, 98-99. See also M. A. K. Halliday, *Learning How to Mean* (London: Edward Arnold, 1975), pp. 17ff. See also *ideational function* and *textual function*.

inventio.   See *invention*.

invention.   In Latin, *inventio*.   The first of the five classical divisions or canons of rhetoric. Invention is concerned with discovering the available means of persuasion in any situation—the finding of arguments. In classical rhetoric, Aristotle defined the basic issues of finding arguments, and these were expanded by Cicero and Quintilian. In modern rhetoric, *invention* is the art of the discovery of subject matter of discourse and is often used synonymously with *prewriting*. Recent developments in the art of invention have been Kenneth Burke's Pentad (*A Grammar of Motives,* [New York: Prentice-Hall, 1945]); prewriting (D. Gordon Rohman, "Pre-Writing: The Stage of Discovery in the Writing Process," *College Composition and Communication* 16 [May 1965], 106-12); and tagmemic invention (Richard E. Young, Alton L. Becker, and Kenneth L. Pike, *Rhetoric: Discovery and Change,* [New York: Harcourt, Brace & World, 1970]). For a complete discussion of invention, its history and role in modern rhetoric, see Richard E. Young, "Invention: A

Topographical Survey," *Teaching Composition: 10 Bibliographical Essays,* ed. Gary Tate (Fort Worth: Texas Christian University Press, 1976), pp. 1-43.

irony. The use of an expression to convey the opposite of its literal meaning; an incongruity between what is expected and what actually occurs. In literature, irony is often used for humor or for rhetorical effect. It is often achieved by allowing the audience or reader to understand an incongruity between a situation and the speeches of characters who remain unaware of the irony. For a bibliography on irony, see Wayne C. Booth, *A Rhetoric of Irony* (Chicago: University of Chicago Press, 1974). Example: "Yet each man kills the thing he loves / By each let this be heard, / Some do it with a bitter look, / Some with a flattering word, . . ."–Wilde, *Ballad of Reading Gaol.*

issue. From classical rhetoric, the subject of a debate, the point of contention in a legal action, or a lesser controversy upon which the larger proposition depends. In "Crucial Issues," *College Composition and Communication* 16 (October 1965), 165-69, Richard Braddock identifies two kinds of issues: stock and crucial. *Stock* issues are commonly relevant issues that can be identified by the questions: Is there a need for a change? Will this proposal satisfy that need? Is there any practical possibility of the proposal being adopted? Is there any danger that the change will introduce disadvantages which outweigh those in the original situation? *Crucial* issues occur between the speaker and the particular audience. See also *status.*

J

jargon. A style of writing characterized by wordiness, abstract terms, euphemisms, cliches, and excessive use of the passive voice; also, the specialized language of a trade or profession.

judicial discourse. See *forensic discourse.*

K

kernel. In transformational grammar, a sentence derived only from transformations which are obligatory, such as verb-subject agreement. For example, "Child plays ball" is a kernel sentence, whereas "Ball is played by child" is not because it involves the optional passive.

L

levels of generality. A principle of writing that refers to the hierarchy of abstraction in a sentence or paragraph, with a high level of abstractness likely in the main clause or topic sentence, followed by movement to lower levels of abstraction or to singular terms. Francis Christensen, "A Generative Rhetoric of the Sentence," *College Composition and Communication* 14 (October 1963), 155-61. Example: "She just bought a new house, ranch-style, rambling, with green shutters and a slate roof." In *Notes Toward a New Rhetoric,* 2d ed. (New York: Harper & Row, 1978), p. 29, Christensen adds this footnote: "Each [level] helps to make the idea of the base clause more concrete or specific, but each is not more concrete or specific than the one immediately above it." See Willis L. Pitkin, Jr., "Hierarchies and the Discourse Hierarchy," *College English* 38 (March 1977), 648-59. William F. Irmscher describes *levels of generality* in *The Holt Guide to English* (New York: Holt, Rinehart & Winston, 1976), p. 84, as "the ebb and flow of sentences in a paragraph between the general and the particular."

linearity. The principle of readability in prose which states that readers should be able to process what they read without having to circle back to reread earlier parts of the text. E. D. Hirsch, *The Philosophy of Composition* (Chicago: University of Chicago Press, 1977), p. 136:

> If the reader must constantly reread clauses, sentences, and paragraphs to construe the writer's meaning, he will not understand or remember that meaning very well. Too much of the reader's effort will have been devoted to construing, too little to understanding the meaning.

linear rhetoric. A type of rhetorical analysis that assumes that discourse is a series of deliberate moves made to achieve a purpose, usually to satisfy the reader about the reasonableness of the writer's point of view. Richard L. Larson, "Toward a Linear Rhetoric of the Essay," *College Composition and Communication* 22 (May 1971), 140-46.

literal term. In a metaphor, the term that is actually being discussed. Laurence Perrine, "Four Forms of Metaphor," *College English* 33 (November 1971), 125-38. Example: "*Wit* is the salt of conversation, not the food."—Hazlitt. See also *figurative term.*

literary discourse. Discourse which focuses on the message itself for its artistic or aesthetic value. See James L. Kinneavy, *A Theory of Discourse* (Englewood Cliffs, N.J.: Prentice-Hall, 1971), pp. 307-92. Examples: short story, lyric, joke, drama, ballad, short narrative.

litotes. A deliberate understatement for emphasis. Example: saying "They seem to like each other" for "They never let each other out of their sights."

locutionary act. Also *utterance act.* The act of a speaker or writer of producing the sounds or graphic symbols with a sense and a reference. J. L. Austin, *How to Do Things with Words* (Cambridge, Mass.: Harvard University Press, 1962), pp. 99-109. See *utterance act* and *speech act theory.*

logos. Also *logical argument.* In classical rhetoric, the means of persuasion by demonstration of the truth, real or apparent. Lane Cooper, ed. and trans., *The Rhetoric of Aristotle* (New York: Appleton-Century-Crofts, 1932), p. 9. See *rhetorical situation.*

M

manipulative domain. The area of educational goals dealing with motor skills.

mathetic function. The function of language for the purpose of learning about reality: identification of the self and exploration of the nonself. M. A. K. Halliday, *Learning How to Mean* (London: Edward Arnold, 1975), pp. 73-75, 106-8: "This is the primary context for the evolution of the ideational systems of the adult language: classes of objects, quality and quantity, transitivity and the like. The context in which these systems evolve is that of the observation of how things are." (p. 106) Examples: the grouping of objects into classes such as household objects or parts of the body, and the introduction of properties than can accompany object names (e.g., blue ball, two pencils).

meaning potential. Sets of options or alternative meanings available to a speaker or writer in a specific environment; what a speaker "can mean," determined by the social structure, with what the speaker "can say" being a realization of it. M. A. K.

Halliday, *Explorations in the Functions of Language* (New York: Elsevier–North Holland Publishing Co., 1977), pp. 43ff. Example from Halliday: A mother wants to reprimand her son for playing at a dangerous building site. She may make a rule based on her authority as his parent, or she may appeal to reason. She may relate the situation to general situations or deal with the particular situation. She may deal with the physical dangers involved (be object-oriented) or she may concentrate on herself or the child (be person-oriented). She may deal with her son as an individual or as part of the family. All of these options constitute the "meaning potential." (p. 51)

memoria. From classical rhetoric, the fourth part or canon of rhetoric that concerns aiding the memorization of speeches. No longer much considered in modern rhetoric.

mental modes. A classification of discourse that includes reverie and persuasion. Leo Rockas, *Modes of Rhetoric* (New York: St. Martin's Press, 1964), p. 219: "Persuasion is abstract reverie, just as reverie is concrete persuasion. If reverie is what the mind privately talks itself into, persuasion is what the mind publicly talks others into."

metalingual. A category of discourse that includes language about language. All grammars are essentially metalingual. Roman Jakobson, "Linguistics and Poetics," *Style in Language,* ed. Thomas A. Sebeok (New York: John Wiley & Sons and M.I.T. Press, 1960), pp. 350-77.

metaphor. A figure of speech in which a word is transferred from its literal meaning to one with which it may be identified. Metaphor differs from *simile* in that neither "like" nor "as" is used. Aristotle calls metaphor of utmost value in both poetry and prose: "It is metaphor above all else that gives clearness, charm, and distinction to the style; and the use of it cannot be learned from without." Lane Cooper, ed. and trans., *The Rhetoric of Aristotle* (New York: Appleton-Century-Crofts, 1932), p. 187. Quintilian calls metaphor the most beautiful of all tropes in *The Institutio Oratoria of Quintilian,* trans. H. E. Butler (London: William Heinemann, 1921), VIII, vi, 4:

> It is not merely so natural a turn of speech that it is often employed unconsciously or by uneducated persons, but it is in itself so attractive and elegant that however distinguished the language in which it is embedded it shines forth with a light that is all its own.

For a recent discussion, see Laurence Perrine, "Four Forms of Metaphor," *College English* 33 (November 1971), 125-38. Example: "Debt is a bottomless sea."—Carlyle.

metarhetorical research. Research that investigates theories of rhetoric and that produces additional theory to describe the properties of adequate theory. Martin Steinmann, Jr., "Rhetorical Research," *New Rhetorics*, ed. Martin Steinmann, Jr. (New York: Charles Scribner's Sons, 1967), p. 25:

> An adequate metatheory does such things as specifying what an adequate theory must explain (exercise of rhetorical ability) and what methods of discovery and verification it must use, and explicating rhetorical concepts like purpose and context.

metonymy. Substitution of an associated word for what is meant. Example: saying "top brass" for "military officers."

mimetic modes. A classification of discourse that is based on the imitation of "human talk" and that includes drama and dialogue. Leo Rockas, *Modes of Rhetoric* (New York: St. Martin's Press, 1964).

model of language. An image of the function of language. As children grow, they expand their understanding of the following set of functions:

> *instrumental*—use of language as a means of getting things done;
>
> *regulatory*—use of language to regulate the behavior of others;
>
> *interactional*—use of language in the interaction between the self and others;
>
> *personal*—use of language as a form of individuality;
>
> *heuristic*—use of language as a means of learning about things;
>
> *imaginative*—use of language to create an environment;
>
> *representational*—use of language to communicate about something; to express propositions.

M. A. K. Halliday, *Explorations in the Functions of Language* (New York: Elsevier–North Holland Publishing Co., 1977), pp. 3-12.

mode of discourse. A category or classification of discourse. Traditionally: description, narration, exposition, and argumentation—first established by Alexander Bain, *English Composition and Rhetoric* (American edition, New York: D. Appleton &

Co., 1890). See each category separately. Recently shortcomings have been pointed out in these categories. See, for example, James Britton et al., *The Development of Writing Abilities (11-18)* (London: Macmillan Education, 1975), p. 4:

> First, it should be noted that they [the traditional modes] are derived from an examination of the finished products of professional writers, from whose work come both the categories and the rules for producing instances of them. The tradition is profoundly prescriptive and shows little inclination to observe the writing process: its concern is with how people *should* write, rather than with how they do.

More recent classifications of modes of discourse are: Philip Wheelwright, *The Burning Fountain* (Bloomington: Indiana University Press, 1968), pp. 59-68: *expressive, poetic, ejaculative, literal, logical, phatic;* James Moffett, *Teaching the Universe of Discourse* (Boston: Houghton Mifflin, 1968): *reflection, conversation, correspondence, publication;* and James L. Kinneavy, *A Theory of Discourse* (Englewood Cliffs, N.J.: Prentice-Hall, 1971): *expressive, referential, literary, persuasive.* For a complete discussion of modes of discourse, see Frank J. D'Angelo, "Modes of Discourse," *Teaching Composition: 10 Bibliographical Essays,* ed. Gary Tate (Fort Worth: Texas Christian University Press, 1976), pp. 111-35.

movements of mind. Plans of organization in discourse that are directly related to patterns and habits in thinking. The analysis of how each paragraph or section of an essay develops the main idea in the whole essay reveals these movements. Richard L. Larson, "Invention Once More: A Role for Rhetorical Analysis," *College English* 32 (March 1971), 665-72:

> If the student, that is, can see how the composers of essays represent their minds moving, pulling together, organizing, and extending data, he may see a range of possible plans open to him in working with his data. He may also understand that a plan for organizing ideas can also be a plan of inquiry—a plan for gathering ideas. (p. 672)

N

narratio. The second part of the traditional argument in which background information is given and the circumstances important to the argument are provided. See *argumentation.*

narration. The classification of discourse that tells a story or relates an event. It organizes the events or actions in time or relates them in space. Relying heavily on verbs, prepositions, and adverbs, narration generally tells what happened, when it happened, and where it happened. Narration was identified as a mode of discourse by Alexander Bain in *English Composition and Rhetoric* (American edition, New York: D. Appleton & Co., 1890). See Leo Rockas, *Modes of Rhetoric* (New York: St. Martin's Press, 1964), pp. 81-111.

nonfinite topics. A set of problem-solving probes that is not considered closed and allows for questions that are not covered by the list. W. Ross Winterowd, "Invention," *Contemporary Rhetoric: A Conceptual Background with Readings* (New York: Harcourt Brace Jovanovich, 1975), pp. 41-42. Example: methods of paragraph development such as analogy, cause and effect, definition, and so on.

O

overdetermination. An overabundance of causes and reasons; an excess of motivating factors. From Freudian psychology. For a discussion of the term's relationship to rhetoric, see Richard M. Coe, "Rhetoric 2001," *Freshman English News* 3 (Spring 1974), 3.

Oxford philosophers. A group of philosophers of language who contend that because hypothetical and mathematical models are too limited for language analysis, the proper place for analysis is found in the meanings and structures of ordinary language as it is actually spoken or written. Led by Ludwig Wittgenstein— *Philosophical Investigations* (New York: Macmillan Co., 1953)— the group includes Gilbert Ryle and J. L. Austin. For application of their ideas to composition theory, see Frank Rice and Paul Olson, *A Curriculum in English* (Lincoln: University of Nebraska Press, 1970-73).

oxymoron. A rhetorical figure in which two contradictory terms are brought together. Example: "deafening silence."

P

paradigmatic analysis. The structural analysis of a text in which a paradigm or overall pattern or schema is formed by extracting certain sentences or other linguistic elements from their sequential order. The analysis is based on semantic or syntactic repetition that seems to be related to the conceptual pattern. The analysis may use the original sentences, may recast the sentences into simpler form using transformational analysis (such as passive to active), or may use sentence paraphrases. Claude Lévi-Strauss used this technique in analyzing recurring patterns in myth. Frank J. D'Angelo, in *A Conceptual Theory of Rhetoric* (Cambridge, Mass.: Winthrop Publishing Co., 1975), chap. 6, uses the technique to determine the underlying organizational pattern of complete essays, and he points out that the underlying patterns, such as definition, classification, partition, exemplification, enumeration, etc., resemble those found in traditional composition texts.

paragraph. A description of a unit of prose involving unity of thought and purpose and usually the presence of several sentences. Alexander Bain is believed to have first developed the rules for the construction of paragraphs. See Paul C. Rodgers, Jr., "Alexander Bain and the Rise of the Organic Paragraph," *Quarterly Journal of Speech* 51 (December 1965), 399-408. For the history of the paragraph and a discussion of recent theory, see Virginia Burke, "The Paragraph: Dancer in Chains," *Rhetoric: Theories for Application,* ed. Robert M. Gorrell (Champaign, Ill.: NCTE, 1967), pp. 37-44, and Virginia Burke, *The Paragraph in Context* (Indianapolis: Bobbs-Merrill, 1969). Francis Christensen, in "A Generative Rhetoric of the Paragraph," *College Composition and Communication* 16 (October 1965), 144-56, defines the paragraph as a "sequence of structurally related sentences" related by coordination, subordination, or a mixture of the two. For a synthesis of recent theory about paragraphs, see "Symposium on the Paragraph," *College Composition and Communication* 17 (May 1966), 60-87. See also Richard L. Larson, "Structure and Form in Non-Fiction Prose," *Teaching Composition: 10 Bibliographical Essays,* ed. Gary Tate (Fort Worth: Texas Christian University Press, 1976), pp. 63-71.

paragraph bloc. A group of paragraphs that work together to develop a major segment of thought in a piece of discourse; one of the main points, closely resembling a major heading in an outline, that is being developed in an essay. William F. Irmscher, *The Holt Guide to English* (New York: Holt, Rinehart & Winston, 1976), pp. 99-102:

The paragraph bloc is a unit of discourse that has not been given adequate recognition or study until recently. Its meaning is closely related to the political use of the word *bloc*. In politics, a bloc is a group of people who work together for some common cause. In discourse, a bloc is a group of paragraphs that work together to develop a major segment of thought. (p. 100)

See *discourse bloc.*

particle. One of the three perspectives of tagmemic invention that views data as discrete contrastive bits. Kenneth L. Pike, "Language as Particle, Wave, and Field," *Texas Quarterly* 2 (Summer 1959), 37-54. See also Richard E. Young and Alton L. Becker, "Toward a Modern Theory of Rhetoric: A Tagmemic Contribution," *Harvard Educational Review* 35 (Fall 1965), 450-68. For elaboration of the tagmemic contribution to composition, see Young, Becker, and Pike, *Rhetoric: Discovery and Change* (New York: Harcourt, Brace & World, 1970). For example, a *particle* description of a tree would emphasize the features that distinguish it from other trees. See also *field, wave,* and *tagmemic invention.*

partitio. The fourth part of the traditional argument that divides the argument into the steps that will be followed in support or illustration of the proposition. Example: "Three reasons can be seen why the parking lot should be removed." See *argumentation.*

pathos. Also *emotional argument*. The means of persuasion in classical rhetoric that appeals to the audience's emotions. Lane Cooper, ed. and trans., *The Rhetoric of Aristotle* (New York: Appleton-Century-Crofts, 1932), p. 9: "Secondly, persuasion is effected through the audience, when they are brought by the speech into a state of emotion; for we give very different decisions under the sway of pain or joy, and liking or hatred." See *rhetorical situation.*

pedagogical rhetorical research. Research that investigates the ability to teach oral and written composition and that produces theories about teaching rhetorical ability. Martin Steinmann, Jr., "Rhetorical Research," *New Rhetorics,* ed. Martin Steinmann, Jr. (New York: Charles Scribner's Sons, 1967), pp. 25-26.

pedagogical stylistics. Teaching students to develop style in writing. W. Ross Winterowd, "Style," *Contemporary Rhetoric:*

A Conceptual Background with Readings (New York: Harcourt Brace Jovanovich, 1975), pp. 253-70.

Pentad. In rhetoric, the set of five problem-solving probes developed by Kenneth Burke which answer the following questions concerning a thought or event: What was done (act)? When and where was it done (scene)? Who did it (agent)? How was it done (agency)? and Why was it done (purpose)? This dialectic method can serve as a heuristic for composition, both as a set of inventive procedures and as a structural pattern for some kinds of writing. As Burke explains—in "Questions and Answers about the Pentad," *College Composition and Communication,* 29 (December 1978), 330-35; and *A Grammar of Motives* (New York: Prentice-Hall, 1945)—he is concerned with a literary theory that views language as a mode of action, as "dramatistic." In *The Holt Guide to English* (New York: Holt, Rinehart & Winston, 1976, pp. 29-30), William F. Irmscher identifies the questions raised by act, agent, scene, means, and purpose as a way of gathering resources for writing. In *The Contemporary Writer* (New York: Harcourt Brace Jovanovich, 1975, pp. 82-89), W. Ross Winterowd illustrates how to apply those questions to an already existing text: What does it say? Who wrote it? In what source was it published? What is its purpose?

Two important articles have appeared recently that help apply the Pentad to the teaching of writing. In "Burke for the Composition Class," *College Composition and Communication* 28 (December 1977), 348-51, Philip M. Keith illustrates how Burke's theory can help place the teacher in a dialectical situation with a student's paper. Joseph Comprone, in "Kenneth Burke and the Teaching of Writing," *College Composition and Communication* 29 (December 1978), 336-40, points out that the Pentad can place writers in the context of agents acting on an audience through words. Prewriting could concentrate on the agent and scene as they move toward formulating purposes. The first draft could consider scene, agency, and agent and could answer questions provoked by the Pentad. Finally, in revision and editing, the Pentad could provide a systematic reconsideration.

performance. A person's actual use of language, which involves factors other than just the internalized set of linguistic rules governing the language. Other factors involved in performance are the beliefs of the speaker concerning the situation and principles of cognitive structure such as memory restrictions.

Noam Chomsky, appendix to Eric Lenneberg's *Biological Foundations of Language* (New York: John Wiley & Sons, 1967); reprinted in Chomsky's *Language and Mind* (New York: Harcourt Brace Jovanovich, 1972), pp. 115-60. See also *competence.*

performance utterance. A type of discourse in which the issuing of the utterance is also the performing of an action. J. L. Austin, *How to Do Things with Words* (Cambridge, Mass.: Harvard University Press, 1962), p. 6. Examples: "I bet." "I name this ship the *Queen Mary.*"

periphrasis. Substitution of a descriptive word or phrase for a proper noun. For example, the Denver Broncos are called the "Orange Crush."

perlocutionary act. The effect on the hearer or reader brought about by speaking or writing; for example, convincing, persuading, misleading. J. L. Austin, *How to Do Things with Words* (Cambridge, Mass.: Harvard University Press, 1962), p. 101. See *speech act theory.*

peroratio. The eighth or last of the traditional parts of an argument that serves as the conclusion in which key points are summarized, a major point is stressed, or future action is recommended. See *argumentation.*

persona. From the Latin *persona* for mask. In rhetoric or literature, the voice or mask that the author puts on for a particular purpose; the created character who speaks to the reader and who may or may not bear resemblance to the real author. For a discussion of *persona,* see Walker Gibson, *Persona: A Style Study for Readers and Writers* (New York: Random House, 1969):

> We use the word, then, in a metaphorical sense—it is as if the author, as he "puts on his act" for a reader, wore a kind of disguise, taking on, for a particular purpose, a character who speaks to the reader. This persona may or may not bear considerable resemblance to the real author, sitting there at his typewriter; in any case, the created speaker is certainly less complex than his human inventor. (p. 3)

personification. The act of attributing human qualities or attributes to an animal or inanimate object. Example: "The greyey'd morn smiles on the frowning night, / Chequering the eastern clouds with streaks of light."—Shakespeare, *Romeo and Juliet,* act II, scene 3.

persuasive discourse. The kind of discourse primarily focused on the receiver of the message, attempting to elicit a specific action, emotion, or conviction. From the time of Corax, classical rhetoric was traditionally thought of as the art of persuasion. For a complete discussion, see James L. Kinneavy, *A Theory of Discourse* (Englewood Cliffs, N.J.: Prentice-Hall, 1971), pp. 211-301. Examples: political speeches, religious sermons, legal oratory, advertising.

phatic communion. The nonreferential use of language for the purpose of contact; ritualized formulas that prolong communication, attract the attention of the listener, or sustain his or her attention. Bronislaw Malinowski, "The Problem of Meaning in Primitive Languages," supplement to C. K. Ogden and I. A. Richards, *The Meaning of Meaning* (New York: Harcourt, Brace & Co., 1927), pp. 296-336. Elaborated in Roman Jakobson, "Linguistics and Poetics," *Style in Language*, ed. Thomas A. Sebeok (New York: John Wiley & Sons and M.I.T. Press, 1960), pp. 350-77. Example: "Hello, how are you?"

planning. The act of oral and written establishment of elements and parameters either before or during writing. Prewriting occurs once, but planning occurs many times. Janet Emig, *The Composing Processes of Twelfth Graders*, Research Report No. 13 (Urbana, Ill.: NCTE, 1971), p. 39.

plurisignation. The characteristic of a symbol in expressive discourse of having more than one legitimate reference; that is, the tendency of symbols to have multiple meanings. Philip Wheelwright, *The Burning Fountain* (Bloomington: Indiana University Press, 1968), pp. 81-86.

poetic function. The function of language which focuses on the message for its own sake; the message itself is its sole purpose. Since classical times, *poetic* has referred to the body of principles concerning the nature of poetry. Today it is often used in reference to the "aesthetic principles" of any literary form. *Poetic* is part of the scheme of functions presented in Roman Jakobson, "Linguistics and Poetics," *Style in Language*, ed. Thomas A. Sebeok (New York: John Wiley & Sons and M.I.T. Press, 1960), pp. 350-77.

polysyndeton. The use of conjunctions between each word, phrase, or clause. Example: "For what avail the plough or sail, / Or land or life, if freedom fail?"—Emerson, *Boston.*

pragmatic information. The relevance of information to the receiver of a piece of informational discourse; any logical inference which is not obvious to the listener or reader becomes information, and the content of the statement becomes a workable, not just a theoretical, concept. See *informative discourse.*

pragmatics. The study of the *use* of signals of language with their meanings by writers or speakers or by the audience in actual speech or writing situations. Rudolf Carnap, *Introduction to Semantics* (Cambridge, Mass.: Harvard University Press, 1942), p. 9: "If in an investigation explicit reference is made to the speaker, or, to put it in more general terms, to the user of a language, then we assign it [the investigation] to the field of *pragmatics.*" C. W. Morris, *Signs, Language and Behavior* (Englewood Cliffs, N.J.: Prentice-Hall, 1946), pp. 217ff: "deals with the origin, uses, and effects of signs within the behavior [speaking and writing situations] in which they occur." (p. 219)

presence. The psychological factor in argumentation of making present to the sensibilities of the audience those elements considered important to the argument. *Presence* is determined by selecting certain elements and presenting them, thereby implying their importance. The speaker/writer focuses on the attitude to be adopted and distracts the hearer/reader from other matters. Chaim Perelman and L. Olbrechts-Tyteca, *The New Rhetoric,* trans. John Wilkinson and Purcell Weaver (Notre Dame, Ind.: University of Notre Dame Press, 1969), pp. 115-20:

> Accordingly one of the preoccupations of a speaker is to make present, by verbal magic alone, what is actually absent but what he considers important to his argument or, by making them more present, to enhance the value of some of the elements of which one has actually been made conscious. (p. 117)

For further discussion, see Thomas F. Mader, "On Presence in Rhetoric," *College Composition and Communication* 24 (December 1973), 375-81.

prewriting. The activity of the mind before writing, evoking ideas, plans, and designs and imposing patterns upon experience. Prewriting is coaxed by journal-keeping, analogy (recognizing relationships among concrete observations), and meditation. Prewriting contrasts with *invention* in that the goal of prewriting is self-actualization, whereas traditionally the goal of invention is to find the means of persuasion. D. Gordon Rohman, "Pre-Writing: The Stage of Discovery in the Writing Process," *College Composition and Communication* 16 (May 1965), 106-12: "Pre-writing we defined as the stage of discovery in the writing process when a person assimilates his 'subject' to himself." (p. 106)

Janet Emig, *The Composing Processes of Twelfth Graders,* Research Report No. 13 (Urbana, Ill.: NCTE, 1971), p. 39:

> Prewriting is that part of the composing process that extends from the time a writer begins to perceive selectively certain features of his inner and/or outer environment with a view to writing about them—usually at the instigation of a stimulus—to the time when he first puts words or phrases on paper elucidating that perception.

process. One of the patterns of thought about a subject that investigates the steps or operations or the course of action to be followed in bringing about a particular result or conclusion. Process discourse is discourse that recounts these steps or activities; it answers the question, How did it happen? or How does it work? See Frank J. D'Angelo, *A Conceptual Theory of Rhetoric* (Cambridge, Mass.: Winthrop Publishing Co., 1975), pp. 45-46. Examples: how to care for African violets; how Cubism was created.

progressive form. See *qualitative progression* and *syllogistic progression.*

progymnasmata. From classical rhetoric, sets of preparatory exercises in speaking and writing used in Roman schools and in the schools of the Middle Ages and the Renaissance. The sets lead students progressively into an introduction to deliberative, judicial, and epideictic discourse. For an example, see Raymond E. Nadeau, *"The Progymnasmata of Aphthonius* in Translation," *Speech Monographs* 19 (November 1952), 264-85.

proleptic device. A word or phrase that integrates elements of prose. E. D. Hirsch, *The Philosophy of Composition* (Chicago: University of Chicago Press, 1977), p. 153. Examples: "but," "similarly," "also," "on the other hand," "however," and so on.

pronuntiatio. The fifth part or canon of classical rhetoric concerned with skill in delivering speeches.

propositio. The third part of the traditional argument, in which the point to be made, the proposition to be proved, or the thesis of the argument is specified. See *argumentation.*

propositional act. The act of uttering words in sentences for the purpose of referring or predicating. John R. Searle, *Speech Acts* (Cambridge: At the University Press, 1969), pp. 24-25:

> The first upshot of our preliminary reflections, then, is that . . . a speaker is characteristically performing at least three distinct kinds of acts:
>
> a. the uttering of words (morphemes, sentences);
> b. referring and predicating;
> c. stating, questioning, commanding, promising, etc.
>
> Let us assign names to these under the general heading of speech acts:
>
> a. Uttering words (morphemes, sentences) = performing *utterance acts.*
> b. Referring and predicating = performing *propositional acts.*
> c. Stating, questioning, commanding, promising, etc. = performing *illocutionary acts.* (pp. 23-24)

See also *speech act theory.*

pseudostatement. Discourse intended to organize the attitudes of the hearer or reader. A *statement,* by contrast, has truth-value. These two classifications of discourse follow the fundamental classical distinctions between scientific, or referential, discourse and poetic, or expressive, discourse which employs emotive statements. I. A. Richards, *Science and Poetry* (London: Kegan Paul, Trench, Trulner & Co., 1935), pp. 61-74.

publication. In rhetoric, a classification of discourse that engages a speaker or writer in impersonal communication with a large anonymous audience that may be remote from the speaker or writer in time or space or both. James Moffett, *Teaching the Universe of Discourse* (Boston: Houghton Mifflin Co., 1968), p. '33. Examples: books, magazines, newspapers, pamphlets, broadcasts.

purpose. The element of the dramatistic framework called the Pentad—act, scene, agent, agency, and purpose—that answers the question, Why was it done? for a thought or an event. Kenneth Burke, *A Grammar of Motives* (New York: Prentice-Hall, 1945), pp. 275-320. See *dramatistic framework* and *Pentad.*

Q

qualitative progression. A type of form in which the presence of one quality prepares the reader for the introduction of another;

one state of mind is appropriately followed by the next. Kenneth Burke, *Counter-Statement* (New York: Harcourt, Brace & Co., 1931), pp. 158-59. Example: T. S. Eliot's *The Waste Land:* from "Ta ta. Goonight. Goonight." to "Good night, ladies, good night, sweet ladies, good night, good night."

R

readability formula. A formula for measuring the readability of prose based upon length of words and sentences, level of human interest, etc. For example, the formula developed by Rudolf Flesch in *The Art of Readable Writing* (New York: Harper & Row, 1949; rev. ed., 1974, pp. 247-51) has two components: (1) a human interest rating that measures the percentages of personal words (proper nouns, personal pronouns) and personal sentences (dialogues, questions, commands, requests, incomplete sentences); and (2) a reading-ease rating (the length of words and sentences).

reality. In the communication triangle, that to which the message refers. For a diagram of the triangle, see James L. Kinneavy, *A Theory of Discourse* (Englewood Cliffs, N.J.: Prentice-Hall, 1971), p. 19.

referend. In discourse, a word that refers to a meaning.

referent. The reality to which the message refers in discourse. C. K. Ogden and I. A. Richards, *The Meaning of Meaning* (New York: Harcourt, Brace & Co., 1927), pp. 9ff.

referential congruity. An organic and interactive relationship of words (vehicle) to their underlying ideas or meanings (tenor) in which there is a mutual participation that opens up or limits the sense of meaning, often, though not necessarily, achieved through imitation. A concrete situation is more closely presented by an imitative vehicle than by conventional symbols. Philip Wheelwright, *The Burning Fountain* (Bloomington: Indiana University Press, 1968), pp. 76-78. Example: the congruity of "fog and filthie air" with the dramatic and moral role of the Weird Sisters in *Macbeth.*

referential discourse. A classification of discourse that has the purpose of conveying information. For a schema of discourse, see Roman Jakobson, "Linguistics and Poetics," *Style in Lan-*

guage, ed. Thomas A. Sebeok (New York: John Wiley & Sons and M.I.T. Press, 1960), pp. 350-77. Referential discourse has been subdivided by James L. Kinneavy to include *scientific discourse, informative discourse,* and *exploratory discourse.* See each of these. See also James L. Kinneavy, *A Theory of Discourse* (Englewood Cliffs, N.J.: Prentice-Hall, 1971), pp. 73-210.

reflection. The classification of discourse that engages a writer in communication with himself or herself. James Moffett, *Teaching the Universe of Discourse* (Boston: Houghton Mifflin Co., 1968), p. 33. Example: a diary or a meditation.

reflexive writing. The classification of writing that focuses on the writer's thoughts and feelings concerning his or her experiences. Janet Emig, *The Composing Processes of Twelfth Graders,* Research Report No. 13 (Urbana, Ill.: NCTE, 1971), p. 4: "the chief audience is the writer himself; the domain explored is often the affective; the style is tentative, personal, and exploratory." See also *extensive writing.*

relative readability. The stylistic principle that one prose style is better than another when it communicates the same meanings as the other does but requires less effort from the reader. Citing its origins in the stylistic theories of Herbert Spencer in *The Philosophy of Style* (1852), E. D. Hirsch gives the principle extensive treatment in *The Philosophy of Composition* (Chicago: University of Chicago Press, 1977), definition, p. 9; discussion, chap. 4.

repetition. A rhetorical figure in which words, phrases, or ideas are reiterated or reworded for the purpose of emphasis or clarity. Repetition is employed in poetry of all kinds. An example in prose would be: "It is defeat that turns bone to flint; it is defeat that turns gristle to muscle; it is defeat that makes men invincible."—Henry Ward Beecher, *Royal Truths.*

repetitive form. Also *repetition.* A restatement of the same thing in different ways, leading the reader to feel more or less consciously the underlying principle. Kenneth Burke, *Counter-Statement* (New York: Harcourt, Brace & Co., 1931), p. 159. Examples: a succession of images; a character repeating his or her identity in changing situations; the sustaining of an attitude; the rhythmic regularity of blank verse.

Frank J. D'Angelo has identified repetition as a major inventive and structural principle in *A Conceptual Theory of Rhetoric* (Cambridge, Mass.: Winthrop Publishing Co., 1975, pp. 46, 142). He describes two types of repetition influencing *style:* syntactic repetition of clauses and phrases in balanced, parallel order; and repetition of identical words and phrases. As a *logical topic,* he divides repetition into *iteration* (repeated statement of an idea or restatement of the idea in another form), *negation* (statement of the idea in its negative or opposite form), and *alternation* (moving between iteration and negation).

representation. In learning theory, the psychological process of learning by which persons free themselves from present stimuli and conserve past experience in a mental model, and the rules which govern storing and retrieving information from this model. Representation is accomplished through action (enactive representation), through visual or sensory organization and summarizing images (iconic representation), and through words or language (symbolic representation). Jerome S. Bruner, *Toward a Theory of Instruction* (Cambridge, Mass.: Harvard University Press, Belknap Press, 1966), p. 10. See also *enactive representation, iconic representation,* and *symbolic representation.*

restricted code. Speech forms which are tied to a particular local relationship and social structure, with meanings that are so provincial that they reduce the contact of the users to those who share a similar contextual history. Users of restricted codes are limited in their cultural and social mobility. Basil Bernstein, "Language, Socialization and Subcultures," *Language and Social Context,* ed. Pier Paolo Giglioli (Baltimore: Penguin Books, 1972), pp. 163-64. See also *elaborated code.*

retroduction. See *abduction.*

rhetoric. In the classical tradition, the art of persuasion; in modern times extended to the art of using language in a way to produce a desired result in an audience (often including *belles lettres*). *Rhetoric* can refer to the qualities of a piece of prose, the body of knowledge about how language works, the techniques whereby discourse accomplishes its ends, or even the body of principles for composition. For a discussion of recent definitions of *rhetoric,* see Robert M. Gorrell, "Introduction," *Rhetoric: Theories for Application,* ed. Robert M. Gorrell (Champaign, Ill.: NCTE, 1967), pp. 1-4. Some current definitions are:

a. "the study of the elements used in literature and public speaking, such as content, structure, cadence, and style. . . ." —*American Heritage Dictionary.*

b. "a study of selection among available means of discourse. . . ." —Gorrell, *Rhetoric: Theories for Application,* p. 3.

c. "The word *rhetoric* can be traced back ultimately to the simple assertion *I say (eirō* in Greek). Almost anything related to the act of saying something to someone—in speech or in writing—can conceivably fall within the domain of rhetoric as a field of study: phonetics, grammar, the process of cognition, language acquisition, perception, penmanship, social relations, persuasive strategies, stylistics, logic, and so on." —Richard E. Young, Alton L. Becker, and Kenneth L. Pike, *Rhetoric: Discovery and Change* (New York: Harcourt, Brace & World, 1970), p. 1.

d. "Rhetoric has meant the art of persuasion, of decoration, and of composition. The first meaning is classical, the second medieval and Renaissance, the third modern."—Leo Rockas, *Modes of Rhetoric* (New York: St. Martin's Press, 1964), p. ix.

e. "Rhetoric is the study of honest, effective communication." —W. Ross Winterowd, *Rhetoric and Writing* (Boston: Allyn and Bacon, 1965), p. 8.

f. "Acting on another through words. . . ."—James Moffett, "Rationale for a New Curriculum in English," *Rhetoric: Theories for Application* (Champaign, Ill.: NCTE, 1967), p. 114.

g. "In short, rhetoric is a mode of altering reality, not by the direct application of energy to objects, but by the creation of discourse which changes reality through the mediation of thought and action."—Lloyd Bitzer, "The Rhetorical Situation," *Philosophy and Rhetoric* 1 (January 1968), 4.

See also *classical rhetoric.*

rhetorical choices. Decisions made consciously about the use of language, such as significant lexical choices, word order for emphasis, kinds of sentence arrangements, logical ordering of the parts of the discourse. Louis T. Milic, "Rhetorical Choice and Stylistic Option," *Literary Style: A Symposium,* ed. Seymour Chatman (London: Oxford University Press, 1971), p. 85.

rhetorical criticism. Research that investigates historically given utterances and produces information about the exercise of rhetorical ability and the relationship of the utterances to the theories of rhetoric. Martin Steinmann, Jr., "Rhetorical Research," *New Rhetorics,* ed. Martin Steinmann, Jr. (New York: Charles Scribner's Sons, 1967), p. 26:

> For a given utterance (Lincoln's Gettysburg address, say, or Dr. Johnson's Preface to his Shakespeare), it shows (not simply recognizes) whether that utterance is a product of exercise of rhetorical ability, or (what comes to the same thing) whether it conforms to the rules of some theory of rhetoric.

See Edwin Black, *Rhetorical Criticism: A Study in Method* (Madison: University of Wisconsin Press, 1965, 1978); and Wayne C. Booth, *The Rhetoric of Fiction* (Chicago: University of Chicago Press, 1961).

rhetorical dualism. See *dualism.*

rhetorical research. See *basic rhetorical research, comparative rhetorical research, historical rhetorical research, metarhetorical research,* and *pedagogical rhetorical research.*

rhetorical situation. The situation of a piece of discourse involving its audience, the problem that elicits the discourse, and the constraints on the writer and the audience, all of which determine which of the available means of persuasion will be used: *ethos* (appeal based on the character of the speaker or writer), *pathos* (appeal to the audience's emotions), and/or *logos* (appeal through words or logical reason). Lloyd Bitzer, "The Rhetorical Situation," *Philosophy and Rhetoric* 1 (January 1968), 1-14:

> a natural context of persons, events, objects, relations, and an exigence which strongly invites utterance; this invited utterance participates naturally in the situation, is in many instances necessary to the completion of situational activity, and by means of its participation with situation obtains its meaning and its rhetorical character. (p. 5)

Richard E. Vatz, in "The Myth of the Rhetorical Situation," *Philosophy and Rhetoric* 6 (Summer 1973), 154-61, alters the relationship between rhetoric and situations so that the speaker/ writer is responsible for what he or she chooses to make salient. Rather than identifying a situation as being rhetorical, Vatz would say that rhetoric controls the situational response and that situations obtain their character from the rhetoric surrounding them.

rhetorical stance. The position and distance assumed by the speaker or writer in relation to an audience. Stance is adjusted to the audience by style and tone. Wayne C. Booth, "The Rhetorical Stance," *College Composition and Communication* 14 (October 1963), 139-45. Elaborated in *A Rhetoric of Irony* (Chicago: University of Chicago Press, 1974); and in *Modern Dogma and the Rhetoric of Assent* (Chicago: University of Chicago Press, 1974).

rhetoric of assent. The art of discovering warrantable beliefs (that is, good reasons), of assenting to those beliefs to the degree that seems warranted, and of improving those beliefs in shared discourse. Wayne C. Booth, *Modern Dogma and the Rhetoric of Assent* (Chicago: University of Chicago Press, 1974):

> If philosophy is defined as inquiry into certain truth, then what I pursue here is not philosophy but rhetoric: the art of discovering warrantable beliefs and improving those beliefs in shared discourse. But the differences are not sharply definable, and I of course think of the inquiry as in a larger sense philosophical. To talk of improving beliefs implies that we are seeking truth, since some beliefs are "truer" than others. Besides, many philosophers from Cicero to the present have defined what they do precisely as I would define rhetoric. (p. xiii)

right of assumption. A term borrowed from law which is the right to assume that precedents are valid, that forms will persist, and that one may build on what was the past. For elaboration of its place in rhetoric, see Richard M. Weaver, *The Ethics of Rhetoric* (Chicago: Henry Regnery Co., 1953), p. 169.

Rogerian argument. A type of argument based on the work of psychotherapist Carl R. Rogers that rests on the assumptions (1) that in order to protect his or her self-image a person will refuse to consider alternative arguments if they are threatening; and (2) that this sense of threat must be eliminated in order to change a person's image. In using Rogerian strategy, a writer would convey to the readers that they are understood, delineate the area where the readers' position is valid, and convince them that they and the writer share moral qualities and aspirations. The goal is to get the readers to understand the writer's position in the same way that the writer has understood the readers' position. Carl R. Rogers, "Communication: Its Blocking and Facilitation" (paper delivered at Northwestern University's Centennial Conference on Communications, October 11, 1951). See Anatol Rapoport, *Fights, Games and Debates* (Ann Arbor:

University of Michigan Press, 1960). See also Richard E. Young, Alton L. Becker, and Kenneth L. Pike, *Rhetoric: Discovery and Change* (New York: Harcourt, Brace & World, 1970), pp. 274-83; or Maxine Hairston, "Carl Rogers' Alternative to Traditional Rhetoric," *College Composition and Communication* 27 (December 1976), 373-77.

S

scene. The element of the dramatistic framework called the Pentad—act, scene, agent, agency, and purpose—that answers the questions, When and where was it done? for a thought or an event. Kenneth Burke, *A Grammar of Motives* (New York: Prentice-Hall, 1945), pp. 127-70. See *dramatistic framework* and *Pentad.*

scheme. In classical rhetoric, a departure from the expected pattern of words. Example: *polysyndeton,* the use of a conjunction between each word, phrase, or clause.

scientific discourse. Discourse that consists of a consideration of one facet of an object and the making of certain kinds of assertions (descriptive, narrative, classificatory, and evaluative) about that facet. The assertions must be referential or informative, excluding the emotions of the writer; and the discourse is not intended to delight. For a discussion, see James L. Kinneavy, *A Theory of Discourse* (Englewood Cliffs, N.J.: Prentice-Hall, 1971), pp. 80-89.

scribal act. The pattern of thought and writing responses brought to bear in the writing situation. See Robert Zoellner, "Talk-Write: A Behavioral Pedagogy of Composition," *College English* 30 (January 1969), 267-320.

semantic closure. The principle of language processing whereby constituent words or phrases are perceived definitely as a functional semantic unit only when a phrase or clause is completed. E. D. Hirsch, *The Philosophy of Composition* (Chicago: University of Chicago Press, 1977), pp. 108-119:

> But even if the review process often occurs at the phrase level, with semantic closure being partly achieved before the clause is completed, the process would still be a review process whereby the provisional interpretations of phrases are being continually confirmed or altered in a definite way as the words unfold. (p. 109)

semantic information. The type and quantity of information about reality that a piece of informative discourse gives. This information is measured by its factuality, its comprehensiveness, and the degree of predictability of the information given. James L. Kinneavy, *A Theory of Discourse* (Englewood Cliffs, N.J.: Prentice-Hall, 1971), pp. 92-94: "'Information' is news, and news is the unpredictable, the unforeseen, the improbable." (p. 93) See *informative discourse.*

sentence combining. A method of teaching composition designed to increase syntactic fluency by teaching students to embed propositions within other propositions, thereby increasing alternatives for sentence structures. Sentence combining had its origins in transformational grammar. See Kellogg W. Hunt, *Grammatical Structures Written at Three Grade Levels,* Research Report No. 3 (Champaign, Ill.: NCTE, 1965); John C. Mellon, *Transformational Sentence-Combining: A Method for Enhancing the Development of Syntactic Fluency in English Composition,* Research Report No. 10 (Champaign, Ill.: NCTE, 1969); Frank O'Hare, *Sentence Combining: Improving Student Writing without Formal Grammar Instruction,* Research Report No. 15 (Urbana, Ill.: NCTE, 1973); William Strong, *Sentence Combining* (New York: Random House, 1973); and Donald A. Daiker, Andrew Kerek, and Max Morenberg, *The Writer's Options* (New York: Harper & Row, 1979). Example from O'Hare:

> The slave *cried out for mercy.* (ING)
> The slave threw himself at the sultan's feet.
> The slave had been caught in the harem. (WHO)

The (ING) indicates that *cried* is to be changed to its *ing* form before combining, and the (WHO) indicates that the sentence is to become a modifier beginning with *who* in the combined sentence. Result:

> Crying out for mercy, the slave who had been caught in the harem threw himself at the sultan's feet.

simile. A stated comparison between two things that are not alike but have similarities. Similes, unlike metaphors, use "like" or "as." Example: "He was like a cock who thought the sun had risen to hear him crow."–George Eliot, *Adam Bede.*

simple topic sentence. A sentence that states explicitly the idea of a paragraph. Richard Braddock, "The Frequency and Placement of Topic Sentences in Expository Prose," *Research in the*

Teaching of English 8 (Winter 1974), 287-302. See *topic sentence.*

situation. See *rhetorical situation.*

socialized speech. Speech that includes questions and answers, requests, and information adapted to take into account the demands of a listener. Jean Piaget, *The Language and Thought of the Child,* trans. Marjorie Gabain, 3d ed. (New York: Humanities Press, 1959), pp. 9-11.

sound experience. The response by the reader's auditory imagination to the sounds symbolized or described by a written text; the vocal/auditory effects of written discourse. Richard L. Larson, "The Rhetoric of the Written Voice," *A Symposium in Rhetoric,* ed. William E. Tanner, J. Dean Bishop, and Turner S. Kobler (Denton: Texas Woman's University Press, 1976), p. 24.

spectrum of discourse. A linear model of discourse relating modes of discourse to a sequence of speaking and writing activities. The spectrum moves from an immediate audience to a distant audience, from the present to the past to the future, from interior dialogue to impersonal communication, and from oral to written. The spectrum is as follows:

Interior Dialogue (egocentric speech)			P
Vocal Dialogue (socialized speech)	*Recording, the drama of what is happening.*	PLAYS	O
Correspondence			
Personal Journal			E
Autobiography			
Memoir	*Reporting, the narrative of what happened.*	FICTION	T
Biography			
Chronicle			
History	*Generalizing, the exposition of what happens.*	ESSAY	R
Science			
Metaphysics	*Theorizing, the argumentation of what will, may happen.*		Y

For instruction in both reading and writing, the spectrum could serve as a progressive structure from simple to complex, concrete to abstract, subjective to objective, all based on the fact that development of symbolic expression depends on general mental growth. James Moffett, *Teaching the Universe of Discourse* (Boston: Houghton Mifflin Co., 1968), p. 47.

speech act theory. The theory of language that the complete act of speech will contain four elements: the *locutionary* or *utterance act*—the vocalization of strings of words or morphemes; the *propositional act*—the stating of the subject and predicating of the verb; the *illocutionary act*—the act of informing, ordering, warning, stating, etc.; and the *perlocutionary act*—the creation of an effect on the hearer by convincing, persuading, misleading, etc. For speech act theory, see J. L. Austin, *How to Do Things with Words* (Cambridge, Mass.: Harvard University Press, 1962); and John R. Searle, *Speech Acts* (Cambridge: At the University Press, 1969).

stance. See *rhetorical stance*.

standard English. A set of language habits used in carrying on the major matters of the political, social, economic, educational, and religious life of the United States; yet this particular set of language habits is not more "correct" than other varieties of English. Charles Carpenter Fries, *American English Grammar* (New York: Appleton-Century-Crofts, 1940), p. 13.

static modes. The modes of discourse—description and definition—that lack temporal progression. Leo Rockas, *Modes of Rhetoric* (New York: St. Martin's Press, 1964).

status. Also *stasis*. The proposition, or definition, or crucial issue to be considered in a piece of discourse; that is, the thesis. From the root *sta,* to stand. Richard Braddock, "Crucial Issues," *College Composition and Communication* 16 (October 1965), 165-69. Otto Dieter, "Stasis," *Speech Monographs* 17 (1950), 345-69:

> In Pre-Aristotelian Greek thought, in Aristotle's physical philosophy and in the *meta*physical rhetoric of Post-Aristotelian Peripatetics of the Third Century before Christ, it [*stasis*] was the rest, pause, halt, or standing still, which inevitably occurs between opposite as well as between contrary "moves" or "motions." (p. 369).

stock issues. See *issue*.

story workshop. A method of teaching writing developed by John Schultz at Columbia College, Chicago, that uses a variety of word, telling, reading, and writing exercises of increasing demand. Essentially self-paced, each exercise has a specific goal. The director coaches the students as they engage in oral exercises, telling, and reading aloud. Betty Shiflett, "Story Workshop as a Method of Teaching Writing," *College English* 35 (November 1973), 141-60.

style. From classical rhetoric, *elocutio.* Traditionally, the third of the major divisions or canons of rhetoric having to do with the figures used to ornament discourse. Historically, style has been interpreted both narrowly, as referring only to those figures that ornament discourse, and broadly, as representing a manifestation of the person speaking. A recent definition has been given by Louis T. Milic, "Against the Typology of Styles," *Rhetoric: Theories for Application,* ed. Robert M. Gorrell (Champaign, Ill.: NCTE, 1967), p. 72: "an individual's style is his habitual and consistent selection from the expressive resources available in his language." For a selected bibliography of the recent scholarship on *style,* consult Edward P. J. Corbett, "Approaches to the Study of Style," *Teaching Composition: 10 Bibliographical Essays,* ed. Gary Tate (Fort Worth: Texas Christian University Press, 1976), pp. 73-109.

style machine. A set of sixteen grammatical-rhetorical qualities that isolate style, and the percentage criteria for classifying any passage of prose as "tough," "sweet," or "stuffy." Walker Gibson, *Tough, Sweet, and Stuffy* (Bloomington: Indiana University Press, 1966), pp. 134-36.

stylistic options. Syntactic variables in the process of generating language, such as sentence length, form of noun modification, placement of adverbials, and construction of verb groups, all of which are generally chosen unconsciously, according to habit, and generally below the sentence level. Louis T. Milic, "Rhetorical Choice and Stylistic Option," *Literary Style: A Symposium,* ed. Seymour Chatman (London: Oxford University Press, 1971), p. 85.

submerged metaphor. An implied comparison made in one or two words, usually verbs, nouns, or adjectives. Maxine Hairston, *A Contemporary Rhetoric* (Boston: Houghton Mifflin Co., 1974), p. 106. Example: "He *cut down* the opposing argument."

superordination. The relationship between discourse blocs in which the first bloc presents *species,* the second *genus.* Willis Pitkin, Jr., "Discourse Blocs," *College Composition and Communication* 20 (May 1969), 138-48.

surprise value. In discourse that provides information, the element of unpredictability or improbability that makes the discourse suitable or informative to a particular audience. For example, what would be informative to a sixth grader would possibly lack *surprise value* for a high school student. James L. Kinneavy, *A Theory of Discourse* (Englewood Cliffs, N.J.: Prentice-Hall, 1971), pp. 134-35.

syllogistic progression. A type of form in a piece of writing in which, given certain things, certain other things must follow, the premises forcing the conclusion. Kenneth Burke, *Counter-Statement* (New York: Harcourt, Brace & Co., 1931), pp. 157-58. Example: the form of a mystery story.

symbolic representation. In learning theory, the transferring of experiences into a mental model of the world through representations in words or language. Jerome S. Bruner, *Toward a Theory of Instruction* (Cambridge, Mass.: Harvard University Press, Belknap Press, 1966), p. 10.

symmetry. In logic, a relationship in which the reversal of the terms of whatever is asserted is also true. Morris R. Cohen and Ernest Nagel, *An Introduction to Logic and Scientific Method* (New York: Harcourt, Brace & World, 1934), pp. 113-16. For a discussion of the use of symmetry in rhetoric, see W. Ross Winterowd, *Rhetoric: A Synthesis* (New York: Holt, Rinehart & Winston, 1968), p. 144. Example: "Fred is as sweet as Ted."

synchronic stylistics. The study of a style of a period; the sum of linguistic habits shared by most writers of a particular period. Richard Ohmann, "Generative Grammars and the Concept of Literary Style," *New Rhetorics,* ed. Martin Steinmann, Jr. (New York: Charles Scribner's Sons, 1967), p. 136. For example, writers of the eighteenth century are said to use balanced, compounded constructions. See also *diachronic stylistics.*

synecdoche. A rhetorical figure in which a part stands for the whole or, less often, vice versa. Example: "The great minds of the decade were seated around the conference table."

syntactic information. The words and word strings (that is, the components of information) in discourse. Indexing, abstracting, and extracting are concerned with this kind of information. See *informative discourse.*

syntactic maturity. The level of elaboration in sentences. For the use of the T-unit to determine that level, see Kellogg W. Hunt, *Grammatical Structures Written at Three Grade Levels,* Research Report No. 3 (Champaign, Ill.: NCTE, 1965) and *Syntactic Maturity in Schoolchildren and Adults,* Monograph No. 134 (Chicago: Society for Research in Child Development, University of Chicago Press, 1970). See also Kellogg W. Hunt, "Early Blooming and Late Blooming Syntactic Structures," *Evaluating Writing: Describing, Measuring, Judging,* ed. Charles R. Cooper and Lee Odell (Urbana, Ill.: NCTE, 1977), pp. 91-104; and Walter Loban, *Language Development: Kindergarten through Grade Twelve,* Research Report No. 18 (Urbana, Ill.: NCTE, 1976), pp. 12-15. For the use of "free modifiers" as a measure of maturity, see Francis Christensen, "The Problem of Defining a Mature Style," *English Journal* 57 (April 1968), 572-79. See also *T-unit* and *free modifier.*

syntagmatic structure. The structure of a discourse viewed as a sequence of structurally related sentences bound to each other and to the lead sentence of the discourse through coordination or subordination. Syntagmatic analysis would examine the linear order of elements from one sentence to another and from one paragraph to another. This kind of analysis would describe a discourse as consisting of a certain number of paragraphs containing a certain number of sentences. Frank J. D'Angelo, "A Generative Rhetoric of the Essay," *College Composition and Communication* 25 (December 1974), 388-96. See also *A Conceptual Theory of Rhetoric* (Cambridge, Mass.: Winthrop Publishing Co., 1975), pp. 60-63.

T

tagmeme. The class of grammatical forms that function in a particular grammatical relationship. Alton L. Becker, "A Tagmemic Approach to Paragraph Analysis," *College Composition and Communication* 16 (December 1965), 237-42:

For instance, the grammatical relationship (or function) *subject* can be manifested by a limited number of grammatical forms or constructions, including noun phrases, pronouns, nominalized verb phrases, clauses, etc. Another way of defining tagmemes might be to say that they are spots or slots in a system where substitution is possible, and they include both the functional spot or slot and the set of substitutable forms. As composites of both form and function, tagmemes reflect an important axiom in tagmemic theory: that meaning cannot be separated from form or form from meaning without serious distortion. (p. 237)

See also Kenneth L. Pike, *Language in Relation to a Unified Theory of the Structure of Human Behavior* (The Hague: Mouton Publishers, 1967); Richard E. Young and Alton L. Becker, "Toward a Modern Theory of Rhetoric: A Tagmemic Contribution," *Harvard Educational Review* 35 (Fall 1965), 450-68; and Young, Becker, and Pike, *Rhetoric: Discovery and Change* (New York: Harcourt, Brace & World, 1970), p. 295.

tagmemic invention. A linguistic method of invention developed from the tagmemic approach to language analysis and description that facilitates finding arguments by helping one carry out three activities: retrieval of known information relevant to the problem, analysis of problematic data, and discovery of ordering principles. Tagmemic theory asserts that all language phenomena can be viewed in terms of particles (discrete contrastive bits), waves (unsegmentable physical continua), or fields (orderly systems of relationships). For example, a descriptive passage about a tree might include a particle description (emphasizing the features which make it an individual); a wave description (emphasizing the tree as a moment in a process from seed to decay); and a field description (partitioning the tree into its parts or placing the tree into a classification of other trees in a taxonomical system).

In discovering details relevant to understanding a subject, the tagmemic heuristic suggests varying perspectives for viewing the subject.

1. *Particle.* What are the features of this subject that make it this and not something else (contrastive features)? For example, if one were to write about teaching children to weave, one might ask from this perspective: What is different about teaching weaving to children from teaching them other forms of art? Is teaching weaving to children different from teach-

ing weaving to adults? Is teaching children to weave different from teaching them other activities?

2. *Wave.* How much can this subject vary and not become something else, and what do the variations mean (range of variation)? For example, in teaching children to weave, are there different activities to be pursued each day? What sorts of difficulties might be encountered? What particular experiences might particular children respond to? How might the children's abilities be expected to change from day to day?

3. *Field.* What is the context in which this subject appears (distribution)? Example: What place does the activity of learning to weave occupy in developing children's aesthetic and artistic abilities? Where and when should this learning take place? What sort of physical setup is needed? What is the purpose of learning to weave in children's development? What experiences should children have before this learning can take place?

The three perspectives then can be used as part of an analysis of problematic data to clearly isolate the unknown by classifying and reclassifying the subject as a question of fact, of process, and of relationships. Finally, the three perspectives can be organized into a coherent set of operations for systematically exploring a subject. Kenneth L. Pike, "Language as Particle, Wave, and Field," *Texas Quarterly* 2 (Summer 1959), 37-54. See also Richard E. Young and Alton L. Becker, "Toward a Modern Theory of Rhetoric: A Tagmemic Contribution," *Harvard Educational Review* 35 (Fall 1965), 450-68. For elaboration of the tagmemic contribution to composition, see Young, Becker, and Pike, *Rhetoric: Discovery and Change* (New York: Harcourt, Brace & World, 1970).

talk-write. A method of teaching composition which moves from speaking (the vocal modality) to writing (the scribal modality). Through oral questioning, students are led by the instructor to the assumptions, implications, and logic of what they will write and to increasingly better versions of what they have written. Robert Zoellner, "Talk-Write: A Behavioral Pedagogy of Composition," *College English* 30 (January 1969), 267-320.

temporal modes. The modes of discourse—including narration and process—which involve a time sequence. Leo Rockas, *Modes of Rhetoric* (New York: St. Martin's Press, 1964).

tenor. The underlying idea or principal subject which is the meaning of a metaphor or figure. A metaphor carries two ideas: the *tenor* and the *vehicle.* I. A. Richards, *The Philosophy of Rhetoric* (New York: Oxford University Press, 1965), p. 96. Example: "Vengeance is a dish that should be eaten cold."– English proverb. The *tenor* is revenge long considered after the heat of anger. The "cold dish" is the *vehicle.* See also *vehicle.*

tenor of discourse. The distance observed between the person writing and the field of discourse, that is, the message and the audience. Janet Emig, *The Composing Processes of Twelfth Graders,* Research Report No. 13 (Urbana, Ill.: NCTE, 1971), p. 37:

> Subcategories can be established as well for the register, "tenor of discourse," which concerns the distance observed between the writing self and field of discourse, expressed by the degree of formality observed in the writing itself. Formality or decorum in written discourse can be established by one or more of the following means: lexical choices, syntactic choices, rhetorical choices.

textual function. The function of language that makes discourse possible by creating text. Through this function, speakers make what they say operational in the context, rather than merely citational, like a group of randomly arranged sentences. M. A. K. Halliday, *Explorations in the Functions of Language* (New York: Elsevier–North Holland Publishing Co., 1977), p. 99. See also Halliday, *Learning How to Mean* (London: Edward Arnold, 1975), pp. 17ff. See also *ideational function* and *interpersonal function.*

texture. A descriptive term referring to the additions to the nouns, verbs, or main clauses in a piece of written discourse. "Thin-textured" writing is plain or bare, with few additions to the nouns, verbs, or main clauses; the other extreme is a texture of great density achieved by variety and concreteness. Francis Christensen, "A Generative Rhetoric of the Sentence," *College Composition and Communication* 14 (October 1963), 155-61.

thematic tag. An explicit verbal unit representing many implicit meanings. E. D. Hirsch, *The Philosophy of Composition* (Chicago: University of Chicago Press, 1977), p. 124. For example, in a legal document, a legal tag like *per stirpes* represents a long tradition of legal interpretation.

theoretical stylistics. The study of theories of style, definitions of style, and the place of style in literary studies. W. Ross Winterowd, "Style," *Contemporary Rhetoric: A Conceptual Background with Readings* (New York: Harcourt Brace Jovanovich, 1975), pp. 253-70.

topic. From the Greek *topos* and the Latin *locus.* A way of thinking about a given subject, or a general head under which arguments are grouped for a particular subject. Aristotle in the *Rhetoric* classified topics into special topics that were appropriate to a particular kind of discourse, and common topics. Special topics were lines of argument to be used on each of the rhetorical occasions—deliberative, judicial, and ceremonial. For example, deliberative discourse should concern what is good or advantageous, making happiness a special topic; judicial discourse concerns the special topics of justice and injustice, or right and wrong; ceremonial discourse concerns praise or censure, making virtue and vice its special topics. Common topics included more and less, the possible and the impossible, past fact and future fact, and greatness and smallness. These were expanded to include definition, comparison, relationship such as cause and effect, circumstance, and testimony such as authority. Edward P. J. Corbett, *Classical Rhetoric for the Modern Student* (New York: Oxford University Press, 1971), pp. 107-67. Frank J. D'Angelo has a discussion of the topics as patterns of thought in *A Conceptual Theory of Rhetoric* (Cambridge, Mass.: Winthrop Publishing Co., 1975), pp. 38ff. See also Chaim Perelman and L. Olbrechts-Tyteca, *The New Rhetoric,* trans. John Wilkinson and Purcell Weaver (Notre Dame, Ind.: University of Notre Dame Press, 1969), pp. 83ff. See also *content-oriented topic* and *form-oriented topic.*

topic sentence. The sentence of a paragraph which indicates the scope of the paragraph. Alexander Bain first identified the topic sentence. Recently the topic sentence has been given new definition:

a. "the topic sentence of a paragraph is to the supporting sentences what the base clause of a cumulative sentence is to its free modifiers. . . ." Francis Christensen, "Symposium on the Paragraph," *College Composition and Communication* 17 (May 1966), 61.

b. "Teachers and textbook writers should exercise caution in making statements about the frequency with which contemporary professional writers use simple or even explicit topic sentences in expository paragraphs. It is abundantly clear that students should not be told that professional writers usually begin their paragraphs with topic sentences. . . . While helping students use clear topic sentences in their writing and identifying variously presented topical ideas in their reading, the teacher should not pretend that professional writers largely follow the practices he is advocating." Richard Braddock, "The Frequency and Placement of Topic Sentences in Expository Prose," *Research in the Teaching of English* 8 (Winter 1974), 287-302.

See also *assembled topic sentence, delayed-completion topic sentence, inferred topic sentence,* and *simple topic sentence.*

transactional function. The function of language in getting things done: informing, advising, persuading, or instructing. The transactional function is used to record facts, exchange opinions, explain and explore ideas, construct theories, transact business, etc. James Britton et al., *The Development of Writing Abilities (11-18)* (London: Macmillan Education, 1975), p. 88.

transitivity. A relationship in which, if one relationship is true, another must be true. Morris R. Cohen and Ernest Nagel, *An Introduction to Logic and Scientific Method* (New York: Harcourt, Brace & World, 1934), pp. 113-16. For a discussion of its use in rhetoric, see W. Ross Winterowd, *Rhetoric: A Synthesis* (New York: Holt, Rinehart & Winston, 1968), p. 144. For example, if Bob is smarter than George, and George is smarter than Joe, then Bob is smarter than Joe.

T-R-I. Topic-restriction-illustration–a logical pattern for developing or analyzing paragraphs. The topic contains the idea of the paragraph; the restriction explains or restricts the topic; and an illustration follows. The pattern moves from a generalization in the topic sentence to a set of specifics. Alton L. Becker, "A Tagmemic Approach to Paragraph Analysis," *College Composition and Communication* 16 (December 1965), 237-42.

triadic argument. An argumentative situation comprised of a writer or speaker; the opponent, who is ostensibly the audience; and a third party who is the true audience. Richard E. Young, Alton L. Becker, and Kenneth L. Pike, *Rhetoric: Discovery and*

Change (New York: Harcourt, Brace & World, 1970), p. 273. Example: political debates. See also *dyadic argument.*

TRIPSQA. A schema to describe the form of any expository paragraph: topic (the idea of the paragraph), restriction (explains or restricts the topic), illustration, problem, solution, question, answer. T-R-I and P-S are illustrated in Alton L. Becker, "A Tagmemic Approach to Paragraph Analysis," *College Composition and Communication* 16 (December 1965), 237-42. W. Ross Winterowd shows how TRIPSQA may be used as a set of topics in "Invention," *Contemporary Rhetoric: A Conceptual Background with Readings* (New York: Harcourt Brace Jovanovich, 1975), pp. 43-44.

trope. From the Greek word meaning "a turn." In traditional rhetoric, a rhetorical device that produces a shift in the meanings of words; a figure of speech. Examples: hyperbole and metaphor.

truth-value. The quality of the content of a message for reporting information. For its use in rhetoric, see Richard M. Coe, "The Rhetoric of Paradox," *A Symposium in Rhetoric,* ed. William E. Tanner, J. Dean Bishop, and Turner S. Kobler (Denton: Texas Woman's University Press, 1976), p. 6. See also *exchange-value.*

T-unit. "Minimal terminable unit," a unit for measuring syntactic maturity comprised of a main clause and all full or reduced clauses embedded within it. This objective unit is dependent upon the grammatical skills of the writer, not his or her ability to punctuate correctly or consistently. Kellogg W. Hunt, *Grammatical Structures Written at Three Grade Levels,* Research Report No. 3 (Champaign, Ill.: NCTE, 1965) and *Syntactic Maturity in Schoolchildren and Adults,* Monograph No. 134 (Chicago: Society for Research in Child Development, University of Chicago Press, 1970). See also "Early Blooming and Late Blooming Syntactic Structures," in *Evaluating Writing: Describing, Measuring, Judging,* ed. Charles R. Cooper and Lee Odell (Urbana, Ill.: NCTE, 1977), pp. 91-104. See also *syntactic maturity.*

typology of styles. An arrangement of styles into categories, such as by period (Elizabethan, Victorian, etc.), by kind of influence or derivation (Euphuistic, Ciceronian, etc.), or according to impression (ornate, simple, plain, and casual). Louis T. Milic,

"Against the Typology of Styles," *Rhetoric: Theories for Application,* ed. Robert M. Gorrell (Champaign, Ill.: NCTE, 1967), p. 66.

U

universal audience. One of the audiences toward which argumentation can be directed that consists of the whole of humanity or, at least, of all normal, adult persons. To convince this audience, argumentation must give reasons that are compelling and of an absolute validity. Chaim Perelman and L. Olbrechts-Tyteca, *The New Rhetoric,* trans. John Wilkinson and Purcell Weaver (Notre Dame, Ind.: University of Notre Dame Press, 1969), pp. 31-35.

universe of discourse. In a piece of discourse, the set of relations composed of a first person, a second person, and a third person; a speaker, a listener, and a subject; an informer, a person informed, and information; a narrator, an auditor, and a story; a transmitter, a receiver, and a message. This structure governs the variations in style, logic, and rhetoric. C. K. Ogden and I. A. Richards, *The Meaning of Meaning* (New York: Harcourt, Brace & Co., 1927), p. 102:

> A universe of discourse is a collection of occasions on which we communicate by means of symbols. For different universes of discourse differing degrees of accuracy are sufficient, and new definitions may be required.

See also James Moffett, *Teaching the Universe of Discourse* (Boston: Houghton Mifflin Co., 1968).

utterance act. The act of uttering strings of words. John R. Searle, *Speech Acts* (Cambridge: At the University Press, 1969), p. 24. See *speech act theory.*

V

vehicle. In a metaphor, the figure itself. A metaphor carries two ideas: the vehicle and the tenor, or underlying idea. I. A. Richards, *The Philosophy of Rhetoric* (New York: Oxford University Press, 1965), p. 96. Example: "My cup runneth over."—Psalm 23:5. The *vehicle* is the overflowing cup; the *tenor* is the blessed life. See also *tenor.*

W

warrant. From logic, the part of an argument which authorizes the mental "leap" involved in advancing from data to claim; its function is to carry the accepted data to the doubted or disbelieved proposition which constitutes the claim, thereby certifying the claim as true. Stephen Toulmin, *The Uses of Argument* (Cambridge: At the University Press, 1958). See also Charles W. Kneupper, "Teaching Argument: An Introduction to the Toulmin Model," *College Composition and Communication* 29 (October 1978), 237-41. Example:

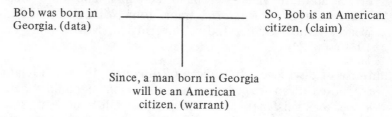

Bob was born in Georgia. (data)

So, Bob is an American citizen. (claim)

Since, a man born in Georgia will be an American citizen. (warrant)

See also *claim* and *data.*

wave. One of the three perspectives of tagmemic invention that views data as unsegmentable physical continua. Kenneth L. Pike, "Language as Particle, Wave, and Field," *Texas Quarterly* 2 (Summer 1959), 37-54. See also Richard E. Young and Alton L. Becker, "Toward a Modern Theory of Rhetoric: A Tagmemic Contribution," *Harvard Educational Review* 35 (Fall 1965), 450-68. For elaboration of the tagmemic contribution to composition, see Young, Becker, and Pike, *Rhetoric: Discovery and Change* (New York: Harcourt, Brace & World, 1970). For example, a *wave* description of a tree would emphasize the tree as a moment in a process from seed to decay. See also *field, particle,* and *tagmemic invention.*

weasel words. The language of whitewash and evasion, used deliberately to conceal unpleasant facts. Mario Pei, *Words in Sheep's Clothing* (New York: Hawthorn Books, 1969), pp. 1-2: "Theodore Roosevelt called these 'weasel words' and with good reason. He did not invent the term, which seems to have first appeared in an article by Stewart Chaplin published in *Century Magazine* in 1900." See Maxine Hairston, *A Contemporary Rhetoric* (Boston: Houghton Mifflin Co., 1974), p. 88. Example: saying "underachiever" for "slow-learner."

written voice. The imagined sound of a writer's voice that readers encounter in every written utterance and that leads them to judge their affinity with, their sympathy for, or their distance from the writer. Richard L. Larson, "The Rhetoric of the Written Voice," *A Symposium in Rhetoric,* ed. William E. Tanner, J. Dean Bishop, and Turner S. Kobler (Denton: Texas Woman's University Press, 1976), pp. 22-32.

Z

zeugma. A rhetorical figure in which one verb governs several words, phrases, or clauses, each in a different sense. Example: "He stiffened his drink and his courage."

Appendix: Lists of Rhetorical Terms by Category

Arrangement

addition
arrangement
assembled topic sentence
bloc
chains of meaning
complementation
connexity
correlation
delayed-completion topic sentence
direction of modification
discourse bloc
dispositio
downplay
enthymeme
equivalence chains
form
grammar of coherence
headword
inferred topic sentence
intensify
levels of generality
linear rhetoric
movements of mind
paradigmatic analysis
paragraph
paragraph bloc
progressive form
qualitative progression
repetitive form
Rogerian argument
simple topic sentence
superordination
syllogistic progression
symmetry
syntagmatic structure
topic sentence
transitivity
T-R-I
TRIPSQA

Classical Rhetorical Terms

anaphora
antithesis
apostrophe
arrangement
asyndeton
cause and effect
classical rhetoric
classification
climax
comparison
confirmatio
confutatio
contrast
crucial issues
definition
deliberative discourse
digressio
dispositio
division
elocutio
emotional argument
enthymeme
epideictic discourse
ethos
exordium
extrinsic proof

71

forensic discourse
hyperbole
inartistic proof
inventio
invention
irony
issue
judicial discourse
litotes
logos
memoria
metaphor
metonymy
narratio
oxymoron
partitio
pathos
periphrasis
peroratio
personification
polysyndeton
process
pronuntiatio
propositio
repetition
rhetoric
scheme
simile
status
stock issues
style
synecdoche
topic
trope
zeugma

Classifications of Discourse

aim of discourse
argumentation
attitude of rhetoric
code
conative function

constative utterance
contact
context
deliberative discourse
description
dyadic argument
ejaculative discourse
emotive function
epideictic discourse
eristic dialogue
exploratory discourse
exposition
expressive discourse
extensive writing
forensic discourse
heuristic dialogue
ideational function
informative discourse
interpersonal function
judicial discourse
literary discourse
mathetic function
mode of discourse
narration
persuasive discourse
phatic communion
poetic function
pragmatic information
publication
reality
referential discourse
reflection
reflexive writing
rhetorical situation
scientific discourse
situation
spectrum of discourse
tenor of discourse
textual function
transactional function
triadic argument
universe of discourse

Communication and Speech Act Theory

addressee
addresser
code
communication triangle
communicative competence
communicative efficiency
conative function
constative utterance
contact
context
correspondence
decoder
ejaculative discourse
elaborated code
emotive function
encoder
exploratory discourse
expressive discourse
ideational function
illocutionary act
informative discourse
interpersonal function
literary discourse
locutionary act
mathetic function
metalingual
model of language
performance utterance
perlocutionary act
persuasive discourse
phatic communion
poetic function
pragmatic information
pragmatics
propositional act
publication
reality
referend
referent
referential discourse

reflection
restricted code
speech act theory
syntactic information
textual function
transactional function
utterance act

General Rhetorical Terms

basic rhetorical research
comparative rhetorical research
discourse
historical rhetorical research
interlocutor
metarhetorical research
pedagogical rhetorical research
rhetoric
rhetorical criticism
rhetorical situation
rhetorical stance
rhetoric of assent
right of assumption
universal audience

Invention

act
addressed writing
agency
agent
cause and effect
comparison
content-oriented topics
contrast
crucial issues
definition
dramatistic framework
enactive representation
existential sentence
extrinsic proof
field
finite topics

form-oriented topics
generative rhetoric
heuristic
iconic representation
implied audience
inartistic proof
invention
issue
nonfinite topics
overdetermination
particle
Pentad
prewriting
process
purpose
representation
rhetorical choices
scene
symbolic representation
tagmemic invention
topic
wave

Linguistic Terms

accessibility
black English vernacular
cant
chains of meaning
channel capacity
code
communicative competence
communicative efficiency
competence
constraint
contact
contextual variation
Crocean aesthetic monism
diachronic stylistics
dialectal varieties
diatypic varieties
elaborated code
equivalence chains

field
figurative term
grapholect
ideational function
impressionism
individualist monism
interinanimation
interpersonal function
jargon
kernel
linearity
literal term
mathetic function
meaning potential
metalingual
models of language
Oxford philosophers
particle
pedagogical stylistics
performance
phatic communion
plurisignation
pragmatics
proleptic device
readability formula
referend
referent
referential congruity
relative readability
restricted code
semantic closure
sound experience
standard English
stylistic options
synchronic stylistics
syntactic maturity
syntagmatic structure
tagmeme
tenor
textual function
thematic tag
theoretical stylistics

transactional function
T-unit
typology of styles
vehicle
wave
weasel words

Pedagogical Terms

affective domain
basic writer
black English vernacular
Bloom's taxonomy
cognitive domain
composing process
conscientization
egocentric speech
enactive representation
Engfish
extensive writing
iconic representation
manipulative domain
pedagogical rhetorical research
pedagogical stylistics
planning
prewriting
reflexive writing
representation
sentence combining
socialized speech
standard English
story workshop
symbolic representation
syntactic maturity
talk-write

Philosophical Terms

abduction
claim
complementation
connexity
correlation

courtship
crucial issues
data
devil term
god term
good reasons
identification
issues
Oxford philosophers
retroduction
right of assumption
status
stock issues
symmetry
transitivity
truth-value
warrant

Psychological Terms

affective domain
cognitive domain
egocentric speech
enactive representation
iconic representation
manipulative domain
overdetermination
representation
Rogerian argument
socialized speech
symbolic representation

Style

accessibility
addition
anaphora
antithesis
apostrophe
assertorial tone
asyndeton
base clause
black English vernacular

cant

channel capacity

code

constraint

contextual variation

core

Crocean aesthetic monism

crot

cumulative modifier

cumulative sentence

diachronic stylistics

dialectal varieties

diatypic varieties

direction of modification

doublespeak

downplay

dramatic *ethos*

dualism

efficient *ethos*

egocentric speech

Engfish

equivalence chains

ethos

exchange-value

figurative term

free modifier

functional *ethos*

generative *ethos*

gobbledygook

grammar of style

gratifying *ethos*

headword

hyperbole

impressionism

individualist monism

intensify

interinanimation

irony

jargon

levels of generality

linearity

literal term

litotes

metonymy

oxymoron

pedagogical stylistics

periphrasis

persona

personification

plurisignation

polysyndeton

presence

proleptic device

readability formula

referend

referent

referential congruity

relative readability

repetition

scheme

semantic closure

simile

socialized speech

sound experience

standard English

style

style machine

stylistic options

submerged metaphor

surprise value

synchronic stylistics

synecdoche

syntactic maturity

tagmeme

tenor

texture

thematic tag

theoretical stylistics

trope

truth-value

T-unit

typology of styles

vehicle

weasel words

written voice

zeugma

Index of Authors Cited

Author

Linda Woodson is Assistant Professor of Rhetoric and Composition, Texas Tech University. After receiving her doctorate in English from Texas Christian University, she taught writing courses and directed the Writing Center at Southern Methodist University. Her publications include contributions to *Contemporary Writing: Process and Practice,* edited by Jim W. Corder (1979).